625
AXL

Dumbarton Oaks

DUMBARTON OAKS

*The History of a Georgetown
House and Garden
1800 – 1966*

WALTER MUIR WHITEHILL

The Belknap Press of Harvard University Press
CAMBRIDGE, MASSACHUSETTS
1967

To the Memory of
ROYALL TYLER
(1884–1953)

Foreword

M OST American cities today are being strangled by the automobile and denatured by haphazard demolition and reconstruction. The case of Washington is sadder than most, for it was conceived with a generous and noble plan that was never fully realized. Today that plan is obscured by ungirdled suburban sprawl, which has turned once rural adjacent counties of Virginia and Maryland into bedrooms for the District of Columbia. Some noble vistas, flanked by fine buildings, persist from the l'Enfant plan of the seventeen nineties, but certain segments of that plan never developed at all, while many that did have lapsed into dreary slums. Yet there are surprising oases, among them one that the city planner Carl Feiss once called "America's most civilized square mile." In an address entitled "Space for Our Congested Cities," Mr. Feiss presented, as a converse to the drabness that afflicts much of the District of Columbia, an area within ten minutes of the White House, at the northern side of Georgetown.

It consists of a series of open spaces joined in a reasonable series of common interests but with different and carefully distinguished uses. At the top of a hill sits Dumbarton Oaks, the handsome mansion in which fine concerts occur. Attached to it is a wonderful little Byzantine Museum, and below and surrounding are some of the most beautiful formal gardens in the country. The Museum and the gardens are open to the public a large part of the year. How many neighborhoods do you know that have their own personal Byzantine museum in them? Below the formal gardens in a hollow is Dumbarton Oaks Park, our excellent, most beautiful and least known wilderness National Park. It is open on weekends and holidays only. It has a little stream winding through it and trails into a bird sanctuary. It is a complete escapist paradise — particularly when the daffodils carpet the little valley and the dogwood is in bloom. People stroll about quietly and relax. On the hill east of and adjoining those two open spaces is a goodsized public park and playground. This is Montrose Park. It has magnificent trees and rolling lawns down which tumble the children from the Jackson School across the street. No urban public school anywhere has a more beautiful play space. Beyond all this and below is Rock Creek Park and an old cemetery which add to the spacious feeling of the entire area.

The Dumbarton Oaks square mile then encompasses the whole range of culture from a wonderful little museum to a wilderness area, all in one neighborhood in the heart of a great city. This is a very unusual oasis of civilization in our savage, modern city.

Dumbarton Oaks, which is the heart of this oasis, and the adjoining National Park, exist as the nucleus of "America's most civilized square mile" solely because Mr. and Mrs. Robert Woods Bliss bought the place in 1920 to achieve what he called "a dream during twenty years of professional nomadism of having a country house in the city." Actually they only lived in this *rus in urbe* for seven years, for Mr. Bliss did not retire from diplomatic service until 1933, and in 1940 they gave the property to Harvard University, which now operates it as a Center for Byzantine Studies. Save for the happy accident of Mr. and Mrs. Bliss's inspiration forty-six years ago, Dumbarton Oaks, like many other spacious nineteenth-century country places within the District of Columbia, might well have been subdivided into house lots or become the site of monotonous high-rise apartment houses.

Dumbarton Oaks is now a learned institution — an integral part of Harvard University — with as good a chance of permanence as anything in this troubled world. Within its walls during the past quarter of a century a group of dedicated scholars have conducted research that has added greatly to our knowledge of Byzantine art, history, thought, and life. Eminent Byzantinists from many countries have been in residence here for periods ranging from a few weeks to many years. Young American scholars have come here as Junior Fellows and remained until they too have become recognized authorities in various fields of Byzantine studies. Throughout the learned world, Dumbarton Oaks has become a familiar name, yet almost nothing has been written that explains the origins of the place.

The Dumbarton Oaks Collection is open to visitors every afternoon except Mondays and legal holidays; so (save in July and August) are the magnificent gardens that surround the house. A liberally illustrated *Handbook* (1955) describes the Byzantine sculpture, metalwork, ivory carving, glass, ceramics, enamels, mosaics, painting, and textiles that are on display. These objects are also being definitively described in a series of scholarly catalogues. Gisela M. A. Richter's *Catalogue of Greek and Roman Antiquities in the Dumbarton Oaks Collection* was published in 1956, while the first two volumes of a *Catalogue of the Byzantine and Early Mediaeval Antiquities in the Dumbarton Oaks Collection* by Marvin C. Ross appeared in 1962 and 1965. A *Handbook of the Robert Woods Bliss Collection of Pre-Columbian Art* (1963) describes and illustrates another remarkable treasure of Dumbarton Oaks. But from these publications — and from the twenty volumes of *Dumbarton Oaks Papers* and the nine volumes of *Dumbarton Oaks Studies* — the visitor will find only scattered clues to the history of the place or to the genesis of the collections. He will not necessarily discover how it is that important Byzantine and pre-Columbian works of art have come to be preserved in a Washington house that stands in gardens that are works of art in themselves.

In December 1964 Mrs. Bliss asked me to write a book that would explain some of these things. She made available to me a painstaking documentary study of the house and its occupants before 1920, prepared for her and her husband a decade ago by Peter G. Vander Poel and by Meredith B. Colket, Jr. (then of the National Archives, now director of the Western Reserve Historical Society). Mrs. Bliss also provided me with an extensive collection of photographs that illustrate the place and its owners at different periods. Since then I have made frequent visits to Dumbarton Oaks in search of additional information.

This little book is concerned only with the house and the land that surrounds it, and with its private owners. It attempts to record the ups and downs of the earlier history of the place and the circumstances that, in the nineteen twenties and thirties, made it what it is today. It became apparent that any attempt even to summarize the varied and extensive scholarly activities of the Center for Byzantine Studies during the past quarter of a century would require a disproportionate amount of space. As Professor Ernst Kitzinger is preparing a detailed history of these for separate publication, I have, for the years since 1940, restricted myself to describing Mr. and Mrs. Bliss's continuing interest in Dumbarton Oaks, and the effect that their collecting and generosity in these later years have had upon the physical character of the property. Thus I leave to Professor Kitzinger's book the story of the research, symposia, lectures, and publications of the Center for Byzantine Studies.

For the period before 1920, I have relied very heavily upon the material assembled for Mr. and Mrs. Bliss by Messrs. Vander Poel and Colket. The rest comes from conversations with Mrs. Bliss and friends. Dr. John S. Thacher, Director of the Dumbarton Oaks Research Library and Collection, and the Honorable William Royall Tyler, Ambassador to the Netherlands, have been particularly helpful. I am grateful to the Virginia Historical Society for permission to quote in chapter III certain of its Beverley papers.

I am grateful above all to Mrs. Bliss for having given me the excuse to become better acquainted with the collections that are framed in this remarkable house and garden, and to learn something of the circumstances that led to their creation. As I have explored Dumbarton Oaks, its contents, surroundings, and uses, I have come fully to agree with my friend Carl Feiss that this is indeed "America's most civilized square mile."

WALTER MUIR WHITEHILL

Boston Athenaeum
2 November 1966

Contents

CHAPTER I

Ninian Beall and the
Rock of Dumbarton

SCOTS have a way of thriving, even after unpromising beginnings. Colonel Ninian Beall (pronounced Bell), the Maryland planter, is a case in point. It is said, without obvious means of proof, that he was born at Largo in Fifeshire about 1630, fought as a cornet of cavalry in the army that David Leslie raised in 1650 to oppose Oliver Cromwell, was captured by the British at the battle of Dunbar, and, as a prisoner, was sold into servitude in the plantations, perhaps in Ireland or the West Indies. However that may be, he was in Maryland in 1658, beginning a seven-year apprenticeship to Richard Hall, the Quaker merchant and burgess of Calvert County. Although this hardly seems the first step in becoming a frontier landowner, as early as 1672 Beall had somehow acquired a three-hundred-acre plantation, Bacon Hall, near the Patuxent River, three miles south of Upper Marlborough in what is today Prince Georges County. There he lived for the rest of his life, although at one time and another he picked up a hundred times as much acreage as he had at Bacon Hall.

Ninian Beall was an efficient fighter of Indians over several decades. As early as 1668, when his apprenticeship was not far behind him, he was commissioned a lieutenant in the Maryland forces; by 1678, when Indian troubles broke out again, he was a captain. By the time he had become a major in 1689, Beall was fighting not only Indians but, as one might expect of a good Scots Presbyterian, the Catholic Proprietor of Maryland, Lord Baltimore. With the fall of James II and the accession of William and Mary, John Coode and others, including Beall, formed "An association in arms, for the defense of the Protestant religion, and for asserting the right of King William and Queen Mary to the Province of Maryland," which marched on the capital of Maryland, St. Marys, and seized the town. The Proprietor's Council moved up the Patuxent to Mattapony, where Coode and his band soon followed them. Articles of surrender setting forth the Protestant cause, drawn by Coode, Beall, and five others, were accepted by the Council on 1 August 1689. The conflict was carried to England, where in 1691 the Associators (including Beall) laid before William and Mary a document entitled "Articles against Lord Baltimore," who was, in the same year, deprived of the government of Maryland although permitted to retain his land and revenues.

In the scramble by Protestants to obtain the government posts formerly held by the Catholic Calverts and their connections, Ninian Beall — by then a colonel — became, in 1692, High Sheriff and Commander in Chief of militia forces in Calvert County, probably as a reward for services rendered during the revolution. When Prince Georges County was created from Calvert and Charles Counties in 1695, Beall was elected one of its first four Burgesses, taking his seat only with the provision that he was free to "goe home and take all necessary Care about the Indians as he sees occasion." As he was still going into the field in command of troops when approaching seventy, the Assembly in 1699, "in remembrance of the many Signal Services and Laborious Endeavours . . . which he still Continues Willingly Even beyond what his age seems capable of," voted Colonel Beall a gratuity of £75, or enough money to buy three Negroes.

During these decades of military and public service, Colonel Ninian Beall was gathering up land wherever he could, much of which he probably acquired through rights obtained by bringing out settlers from Scotland. He accumulated tracts piece by piece, occasionally in the form of small scattered farms, at other times in units large enough to be properly called plantations, like Charles Hill on the Piscataway, Largo, Fife, and Collington. Most of his land was located in the rolling wooded country between the Patuxent River and the East Branch of the Potomac, today the Anacostia River, but he owned property in Caroline County on the Eastern Shore and in Harford to the north, as well as in New Scotland Hundred in Charles County to the west, in what was later to become Georgetown. It is indeed remarkable that a man still apprenticed at thirty, even an industrious Scot, should have succeeded in assembling land grants that totaled some thirty thousand acres.

Through his long years of military service, Ninian Beall became intimately acquainted with the Maryland frontier and the Indian trails traversing it. Thus he came to know the future site of Dumbarton Oaks, and in 1703 added it to his holdings. The land in question was originally part of the Proprietor's Manor of Calverton, which extended from Chaptico Creek on the Wicomico west along the Potomac for an unknown distance. The Calverts had originally set the manor aside for allotment in fifty-acre plots to Indians, with a thousand acres reserved for themselves and some other acreage for English settlers. But as Indians showed little inclination to farm there in an orderly manner, the land was eventually granted to white settlers. The land was surveyed in early November 1703 by Clement Hill, Jr., "Surveyor of the Western Shores," and a patent granted by "Charles, Absolute Lord and Proprietor of the Province of Maryland" in the following terms:

We doe therefore hereby grant unto him the said Ninian Beale, all that Tract or pracell of land called Rock of Dunbarton — lying in the said County. Beginning at the South East Corner Tree, of a Tract of Land taken for Robert Mason standing by Powtomack River side at the mouth of Rock Creek on a point running thence with the said land North West six hundred and forty parches thence East three hundred and twenty parches, then South six degrees and a half, Easterly four hundred and eighteen parches, then West twenty parches, then South South West one hundred and seventy five parches, then with a straight line by the Creek and River to the first bound. Containing and then laid out for seven hundred ninety and five acres more or less.

The land was to be held "in free and Common Soccage," that is without other feudal dues than a rent of £1/11/9½ sterling, to be paid semi-annually at St. Marys on the feasts of the Annunciation and Michaelmas. This 795-acre tract, opposite the little falls of the Potomac, which was as far inland as shipping could go, included a beautiful hill overlooking the river. Thus Beall, who was in the habit of applying Scottish place names to his Maryland holdings, called his new possession after the Rock of Dumbarton, a striking and picturesque formation on the north bank of the Clyde below Glasgow, which had long been surmounted by a castle. The Rock of Dumbarton was one of the standard "sights" of Scotland. Indeed John Slezer in 1693 had devoted three plates to it in his *Theatrum Scotiae: Containing the Prospects of their Majesties Castles and Palaces together with those of the most consider-able towns and colleges . . . all curiously engraved on copper plates.* But with the creative imagination of seventeenth century spelling, where almost any similar consonant or vowel seemed as good as another, Ninian Beall — whose own name was often written with like flexibility — named his new patent Rock of Dunbarton, shuffling in an n rather than the correct m.

Land was, of course, only useful if one could turn it to a profit. Nine years later Ninian Beall almost had a good chance to make something out of the Rock of Dunbarton, when it caught the attention of a Swiss colonizer, Baron Christopher de Graffenried. This native of Bern, with his fellow-townsman Georg Ritter and with Franz Ludwig Michel of the Rhenish Palatinate, had secured an option on 100,000 acres in North Carolina and sent there 650 settlers from the Palatinate and 150 from Switzerland to found the colony of New Bern. As that settlement ran into difficulties, partly from the Tuscarora Indians, de Graffenried turned in 1712 to Governor Spotswood of Virginia for other land. Spots-wood gave him patents for land on the lower Potomac, but when they turned out to be worthless, he went up river, lured by reports of deposits of silver. There much of the land on the Virginia shore was claimed by the Proprietors of the Northern Neck, the Fairfaxes, and on the Maryland shore by the Calverts. But de Graffenried hoped to buy some of this by raising money on the strength of the silver deposits. The region greatly pleased him, for he wrote:

I believe there are scarcely any places in the world more beautiful and better situated than this of the Potomac and Canavest, which we wish to divide into little colonies, the first just below the falls. [There] at the foot of the falls, to the side we wished to build a house and establish a plantation in order to cart merchandise from there. The greatest merchant vessels can sail up to within a half of a quarter of a league of this fall, which is very convenient for commerce.

He spoke of "a very pretty island of very good ground" (Analostan Island) and "facing it, an angle between the great Potomac River and on the other little river named Gold Creek, in French *Ruisseau d'Or*." Gold Creek was, of course, what we know as Rock Creek, and on the angle was the Rock of Dunbarton, which he described as "Plantation of Colonel Bell, eight hundred acres of land to sell for 168 pounds sterling. Very suitable and convenient for our design. From there one goes to Canawest on horseback or on foot. . . . This place and the plantation of Colonel Bell would have suited us well."

Alas, the silver deposits never materialized; without them de Graffenried could not raise the money to buy the land that so appealed to him. He returned to Europe, and when in 1714 he sent over another group of Germans, he had them settle at Germania on the Rapidan River, now in Orange County, Virginia, where land was cheap. This likely sale having fallen through, the Rock of Dunbarton remained in Colonel Ninian Beall's possession until his death in 1717.

In his will Ninian Beall left Bacon Hall, where he had always lived, to his eldest son Thomas. His son George received for his share "my plantation and tract of land called 'Rock of Dunbarton' lying and being at Rock Creek and containing 480 acres with all the stock thereon of cattle and hogs." Why 480 acres, rather than the 795 he had acquired in 1703? Possibly title to the remainder had been clouded by overlapping grants. In any case, three years after his father's death George Beall patented a huge 1,380 acre tract designated as "Addition to Rock of Dunbarton," which seems to have included part of the original grant and additional land on the interior.

George Beall, who was 22 at the time of his father's death, moved to the Rock of Dunbarton after his marriage to Elizabeth, the daughter of Thomas Brooke, and settled on his plantation. His house still stands as 3033 N Street. Within a few years the frontier aspect of the place vanished, for settlers and merchants began to come into the region. In 1738 the Virginia legislature established a Potomac ferry, whose Maryland terminus was not far from the Rock of Dunbarton. By 1751 a settlement at the mouth of Rock Creek had become of enough importance for its inhabitants, among them some Scots merchants, to petition the Maryland Assembly to establish it as a town. The act passed that year, in consequence of the petition, called the place George Town in honor of George II and established a commission of seven members to "buy and purchase sixty Acres, Part of the Tracts of Land belonging to Messieurs George Gordon and George Bell," at prices to be agreed upon between Commissioners and owners or, on failure to agree, by a jury of seventeen. The sixty acres were to be laid out, with suitable streets, lanes, and alleys, into eighty town lots, two of which were to be selected by each of the former owners, Gordon and Beall. Buyers of lots were obligated to build "substantial houses," with at least one chimney of stone or brick, within two years of the purchase. The act further allowed the new town to establish three-day fairs in April and October as "an Encouragement to the back Inhabitants and others to bring Commodities there to sell and Vend."

George Beall took this urbanization of his surroundings in bad part. The petition had carefully been concealed from him. When he heard of it by accident, he went straight to Annapolis, which had by then become the capital, to protest. After wasting some days, having been informed by two members of the upper house that the petition for Georgetown had been rejected, he went home, "well satisfied that nothing could be done that Season of Assembly in relation to the Said petition." His informants were clearly wrong, for the petition went to the lower house and the act establishing the new town was passed in Beall's absence.

Justifiably annoyed, he at first refused to choose the two town lots which were due him under the terms of the act. On 28 February 1752 the Commissioners warned him that "if he did not make his choice within 10 days . . . he could only blame himself for the consequences." George Gordon, the other injured party, had already made his selection. After a week's delay, George Beall grudgingly wrote the Commissioners, "If I must part with my property by force, I had better save a little than be totally demolished. Rather than none, I accept these lots, numbers 72 and 79, said to be Mr. Henderson's and Mr. Edmonston's. But I do hereby protest and declare that my acceptance of the said lots, which is by force, shall not debar me from further redress from the Commissioners or others, if I can have the rights of a British subject. God save the King." He did, indeed, carry the fight to the Assembly in 1753, asking for the repeal or modification of the act of 1751.

Although the Commissioners only took 33⅟₆ acres of the Rock of Dunbarton, George Beall was dissatisfied with the price paid him and the valuation placed upon the two town lots that he had grudgingly selected. He told the Assembly that on his expropriated land there stood "three dwelling houses and a store house," which he rented for "twenty pounds current money and ten pounds Sterling" per annum, and that the "store" contained a room he was using for his own purposes. After mentioning the "rolling house, orchard and Several other Valuable Improvements" on his property, Beall stated that he understood the site chosen for the town would be one that contained no "improvements." He thus alleged "manifest partiality in the Commissioners in laying out the Said town, they haveing Included all your petitioner's improvements and Left the most Valuable parts" of George Gordon's improvements "out of the town tho the same lays near the Center thereof."

Although George Beall had as little success as many twentieth-century householders have with highway departments and redevelopment authorities, the steady growth of Georgetown enhanced the value of the large tract that he still owned. With the prospect of war with France, Governor Dinwiddie of Virginia and Governor Sharpe of Maryland discussed common problems of the two colonies. By 1754 the French had established Fort DuQuesne on the site of Pittsburgh, from which they and their Indian allies could harass the back country of the English colonies and block English penetration into and across the mountains. The valley of the Potomac formed a natural highway in that direction; moreover, Georgetown stood at a vital crossroads on that river. The Governors were chiefly concerned with the transportation of troops and supplies as far west as Fort Cumberland on Wills Creek in western Maryland; such a road would not only serve for possible attack on Fort DuQuesne but for fur trading with the Ohio country. The final decision was to build the road by way of Frederick, a route that proved extremely useful to the merchants of Georgetown. This so-called River Road was the principal route west from northern Virginia and Maryland until the construction of the National Road in the nineteenth century. Along it Braddock's troops marched in 1754 toward their bloody defeat on the Monongahela, those that came from Williamsburg or were landed at Alexandria passing through Georgetown on the way. General Braddock himself reportedly wrote the actress George Ann Bellamy, "Never have I attended a more complete banquet or met better dressed or mannered people than I met on my arrival in George Town, which is named after our Gracious Majesty."

Although in 1752 George Beall stood on the rights of a British subject and interlarded his complaints with "God save the King," in 1776 — aged 81 — he appeared as a major in the Revolutionary forces of Maryland. By the time of his death in 1780 he was belatedly styled, like his father before him, Colonel. He and his wife, who had died in 1748, were buried in a family plot near their N Street house; later, when Georgetown became more urban, their bodies were removed to the Presbyterian Burying Ground.

By the time of George Beall's death, the name of his estate was commonly spelled in the correct Scottish manner; thus his will divided the Rock of Dumbarton between his sons George and Thomas, the boundary being the stream just north of Dumbarton Oaks, described as "the Great Branch of Rock Creek that leads to the Saw Mill thence to the main road." The division of the plantation was later clarified by amicable agreements and deeds between the two brothers. In effect, Thomas, the younger son, received the better and major portion, the land south of the Great Branch. In the attempt to establish the original boundaries of the Rock of Dumbarton, it became necessary to identify the specific tree from which all the measurements of Ninian Beall's patent of 1703 were reckoned. In response to a newspaper advertisement in the *Maryland Gazette*, placed by the commissioners appointed by Montgomery County to determine the boundary, one Simon Nicholls, aged 55, appeared and, "being duly sworn on the Holy Evangels of God," declared that

about 15 or 18 years ago, being on the side of the Potomack River about 8 or 10 yards from the bank . . . somewhat above the mouth of Rock Creek and about 20 yards on the east side of a small branch or gutter leading down to the River he was then and there shown by Luke Bernard Senior this stump of a tree about three or four feet high and he the said Bernard told this deponent that he [Bernard] was shown it when [it was] a tree by John Powel, for the bounded or beginning tree of a tract of land called the Rock of Dumbarton.

Adding his bit to the information, Andrew Heugh, one of the commissioners, swore that "about thirty years ago when he kept store at Rock

Creek warehouse for Messrs Robert and Thomas Dunlap of Glasgow Merchants the late Colonel George Beall was often at the store." When the Colonel learned that his nephew Thomas Edmonston "pretended to take up a piece of land at the mouth of Rock Creek Branch deemed by everyone about the place to be Colonel Beall's land this seemed to give the Colonel a good deal of concern and he showed the deponent a paper containing what either Luke Bernard did or would swear relative to the beginning of his land." Thomas Beall received also his father's houses and lots in Georgetown as well as the tract known as "Conjurers Disappointment." Colonel George Beall further willed "my daughter Elizabeth Evans my negro fellow Jack to serve 4 years and then to be set free."

Following a common custom of Marylanders of his time, Thomas Beall added a patronymic to his name, normally styling himself Thomas Beall of George, to distinguish himself from other Thomas Bealls. Born in 1748, the year of his mother's death, he married in 1773 Anne Orme, who bore him two daughters: Eliza Ridgeley, who became the wife of the Honorable George Corbin Washington, kin of the President, and Harriet, who married a Georgetown neighbor, John Peter. Thomas Beall of George and his family lived in the house that is today numbered 3017 N Street, which was in 1798 described as a two-story brick house with a smaller two-story office house, a brick kitchen, another small one-story brick house, a wooden carriage house, and a granary. During the Revolution he served on a committee charged with carrying out in Georgetown the instructions of the Continental Congress; later he held various public offices in Georgetown, including those of Alderman and Mayor.

Colonel George Beall had sought valiantly to keep intact his patrimony, the Rock of Dumbarton, by raising crops on it. Thomas Beall of George, on the contrary, regarded the portion that he had inherited as a source of profit through subdivision. Within three years of his father's death, a 61-acre parcel of the Rock of Dumbarton was added to Georgetown in accordance with an Act of the Maryland Assembly. Two years later another area, known as the "Second Addition to Georgetown" was similarly alienated. These two additions lay north of the town and east of High Street (Wisconsin Avenue); the first ran as far north as Back (or Que) Street, the second was located above it as far north as Road (or R) Street. Furthermore the many lots sold to individuals, as well as land

on the crest of the Heights above Georgetown, whose transfers are recorded in the courthouses of Montgomery County and the District of
Columbia, provided Thomas Beall of George with a lucrative source of
income for years.

So far as the integrity of his plantation was concerned, Colonel George
Beall had been foresightedly correct in opposing the establishment of
Georgetown. The growth of the adjacent town and, above all, the transfer
of the national capital to the District of Columbia, doomed the Rock of
Dumbarton as an entity. According to Federal land records, by 1798 the
795 acres that Ninian Beall had received in 1703 were reduced to only
eighty. The portion of land on which the present Dumbarton Oaks was
to be built still remained to be carved from this shrunken remnant.

CHAPTER II

William Hammond Dorsey, Builder of the House

O F all the land that Thomas Beall of George had for sale, the most desirable was that on the high ground that came to be known as Georgetown Heights, an attractive area along and above the northernmost fringe of the town. In 1800 it commanded a superb view of shipping along the Georgetown waterfront, the embryonic city of Washington, and the winding reaches of the Potomac. Before the site of the Federal City was definitely selected, eager citizens of Georgetown had urged this one, for, they alleged, "In point of healthiness, goodness of air and water, considerations of so much value, there are few spots in the United States which can boast any advantage over the one in contemplation; and it is conceived that the hilliness of the country, far from being an objection, will be thought a desirable circumstance, as it will contribute to the beauty, health, and security of a city intended for the seat of empire." Although this view did not prevail, Georgetown Heights had a grandstand view over the site of the new capital. Thomas Beall of George consequently was able to sell land along what is now R Street to excellent advantage. Among his purchasers was William Hammond Dorsey, who bought the site of Dumbarton Oaks.

He was the son of Colonel John Dorsey (1736–1810) of Ann Arundel County, who, through his wife Mary Hammond, had come into iron deposits along Curtis Creek, from which he developed a thriving industry, producing, among other things, ships' anchors. He also owned the Baltimore shipping firm of John Dorsey and Company. John's fourth child, William Hammond Dorsey, was reputedly born at Oaklands in Howard County in 1764, studied law, and was, in 1787, admitted to the bar in

Montgomery County, which had been carved out of Frederick County a few years earlier. In March 1790 he married Ann Brooke, the orphaned heiress of Colonel Richard Brooke of Fair Hill, near Olney in Montgomery County. Although Brooke was a Quaker, he had served as an officer in the Revolution and had sent Ann to Mrs. Ann Brodeau's smart finishing school in Philadelphia, with the expectation of seeing her advance *"rapidly* in every female accomplishment," which, he assured her, "will give me more real pleasure than the acquisition of thousands." Certainly her accomplishments were sufficient to catch her a husband, handsome enough to be known as "Pretty Billy." The young couple lived initially at Fair Hill, a wood and brick house that is still standing and is reputed to be haunted by the ghost of Richard Brooke, who rides his horse up one stairway and down another for purposes unknown. The 1790 census shows the Dorseys maintaining a household of 12 whites and 18 slaves there.

After three or four years at Fair Hill, the Dorseys moved to Georgetown, drawn, one suspects, by the charm of real estate speculation. Georgetown and part of Montgomery County had been included in the hundred square miles set aside for the Federal City. Major l'Enfant had laid out a stupendous baroque pattern of avenues, streets, circles, and malls in the meadows that lay across Rock Creek from Georgetown, and sites were allocated for the Capitol, the President's House, and other public buildings. As l'Enfant had looked far to the future, and allowed for the development of a city greater than Paris then was, these buildings were widely separated from one another. Consequently miles of streets and avenues had to be created out of meadows and marshes. This, in theory, could be accomplished by selling lots of land to private individuals and converting the proceeds into public improvements. Once sales were opened there was a mad scramble for desirable sites, but as there were so many, nobody could be quite sure which *were* the most desirable. Thus, through the human cupidity incited by the possession of land that would increase in value if certain political steps should be taken, many highly placed persons, who should have known better, created an orgy of real estate speculation. Even Robert Morris, the respected financier of the Revolution, got into the act, eventually going to jail for his pains, in the company of equally avid but less distinguished persons. Into the real estate boom William Hammond Dorsey confidently plunged, first exchanging his wife's inherited property in rural Montgomery County for Georgetown lots that gave promise of a rapid rise in value, then acting on behalf of New York speculators to buy entire squares in Washington, and finally buying large amounts of Washington land in his own name.

In 1793 Dorsey bought from Peter Casanove for 3,500 pounds three Georgetown lots facing Causeway Street and the river, from Fishing Lane east toward the Creek. He further bought "ground and water rights," extending from one of these lots down to the channel of the Potomac, "as the said channel now runs or may at any time in the future" and there built a wharf, which was probably partly responsible for his future interest in the growth of the Potomac Company. There was, however, doubt as to whether this valuable riverside property belonged to Georgetown under the original survey of 1752. Dorsey was a member of the Georgetown Common Council in 1800 when it appointed him to a committee to look into the matter; he submitted the report which declared that the town indeed had rights to the land.

To develop his property north of Causeway Street, Dorsey ceded to Georgetown in 1797 a strip of land running back from the river for the construction of Jefferson Street, retaining the right to move any buildings he had there. This worked out well, for in the succeeding years he sold about a dozen small lots along Jefferson Street for commercial purposes.

From Thomas Beall of George he bought in 1793 and 1794 about twenty lots, lying between Beall and Dumbarton Streets, in Beall's First Addition to Georgetown, selling most of them soon after. As late as 1806 he bought more land in Beall's Second Addition, bounded by Back, West, Valley, and Congress Streets, on the turnover of which he made a profit of $2,800 in only six months. All this property, of course, lay within the boundaries of the original Rock of Dumbarton plantation.

In Washington Dorsey's speculations were more ambitious and less successful, for the scale was greater and the risks higher. In 1798 he contracted to buy scattered lots in the heart of the present city from David Burnes, a Scot who had made a killing by the purchase of the 225-acre farm once known as Beall's Levels. Burnes's house was on the site of the Pan American Union building on 17th Street. Shortly before Burnes's death in 1799, Dorsey bought at auction 24 squares of land in the city in anticipation of a rise in values which did not occur as fast as he expected. After David Burnes's death his widow and only daughter found themselves handsomely off. Marcia Burnes, as an heiress in this brave new world, made an excellent marriage with General John P. Van Ness, a congressman from New York.

William Hammond Dorsey was active in politics as well as land speculation. As early as 1795 he was chosen Recorder of the Georgetown Corporation and later a member of its Common Council. As he was concerned with the Potomac Company — chartered in 1794 with the active support of President Washington to achieve a water route westward, but beset with many difficulties — any measure that furthered the project greatly interested him because of his holdings of Georgetown waterfront property. Elected a member of the Maryland Senate in 1796, he introduced a bill to "authorize the Potowmack company to receive Tolls on produce carried through the canal at Great Falls," and served on a committee to consider the construction of a turnpike from Washington to Annapolis. The Potomac Company's pioneer transportation system was never successful, for the locks around the two falls of the river, carved out of solid stone, were only ten to fourteen feet wide. Thus only gondolas and small canal boats, carrying 80 to 100 flour barrels each, could use it. The successful Chesapeake and Ohio Canal, which eventually replaced it, could handle boats carrying 1000 to 1200 barrels.

But around the turn of the century Dorsey was still full of optimism, and as his family was increasing, he wished to build a larger house in Georgetown. Having had frequent transactions with Thomas Beall of George, it was to him that Dorsey turned for a site, buying in October 1799 a tract of nine and a half acres in Georgetown Heights. As this on consideration seemed too small for a man of his ambitions, he returned the deed to Beall in July 1800 and purchased instead, for two thousand pounds, twenty acres of Rock of Dumbarton land in approximately the same location. His purchase was on a rolling piece of high ground on the north side of Road (R) Street and east of High Street (Wisconsin Avenue), which included an impressive grove of oak trees. An additional purchase in August 1801 enlarged Dorsey's holdings to 22 acres, the size that the property was to remain for nearly a century. The only name that Dorsey seems to have applied to his purchase was Rock of Dumbarton, thus claiming for his 22 acres the name that Colonel Ninian Beall had applied to his entire plantation nearly a century before. It was a site worthy of a prosperous lawyer and State Senator who, being a man of ambition, anticipated an even greater future for himself in the fast-changing world around him. The site had the finest view in Georgetown; moreover, nearby were such places as Samuel Davidson's Evermay, Benjamin Mackall's Mackall Place, and the house Francis Lowndes was building at Tudor Place, which was later to be rebuilt by Thomas Peter.

William Hammond Dorsey probably began his new house in 1800. Neither plans nor the name of the architect have survived. Like other gentlemen of the time, Dorsey may have been his own architect, working closely with a master carpenter and with architectural handbooks. Possibly Dr. William Thornton had a hand in the design, for that eminent architect and his family were neighbors and close friends. Ann Dorsey and Mrs. Thornton, whose mother was the proprietor of the Philadelphia finishing school at which they had been classmates, constantly saw each other, exchanging garden plants and driving about together to watch the progress on new government buildings that Dr. Thornton had designed.

Whoever designed it, the Dorseys' house was a handsome one, although considerably smaller than today's Dumbarton Oaks, in which it is incorporated. Two stories high, with five bays, and built of red brick, it resembled other great houses of the Federal period, such as White's Heritage on Kent Island, Maryland, reputedly built also about 1800. The distinguishing features were a slightly receding central bay for the entrance, and countersunk panels of stone between the horizontal rows of twelve-pane windows. Similar countersunk panels, not unlike some used by Charles Bulfinch in Boston about that time, are to be seen on the nearby house at 3339 N Street. One can only guess at the form of entrance and shape of the roof, for the earliest surviving view is a photograph taken in the eighteen sixties, which shows a building that already had been considerably modified. Inside was a spacious central hall, running through the house, separating two large drawing rooms, each with its fireplace.

The new house must have been occupied by 24 October 1801, for on that day the Georgetown Corporation received a letter from Dorsey, asking "if his removal to his present place of residence," which was outside the limits of the town, "will disqualify him from service on the Corporation." The answer was that it did not, although Dorsey had earlier in the year lost his seat in the Maryland Senate and a post as Associate Justice of the Montgomery County Court when Congress assumed the responsibility of governing the District of Columbia. On 3 March 1801, the day before he retired from the Presidency, John Adams named Dorsey a Justice of the Peace, thus making him, like another Georgetown resident William Marbury, one of the President's controversial "midnight judges." When Marbury was refused his commission by James Madison, President Jefferson's Secretary of State, he instituted the suit that ended in Chief Justice John Marshall's famous decision in *Marbury vs Madison*, in which for the first time he proclaimed his doctrine of the sanctity of the Constitution. Dorsey had better luck than Marbury, for he received his commission from the new Jefferson administration on 27 March 1801. Seemingly he accommodated himself to the change of party, for on 26 March he was also appointed the first judge of the Orphans Court in the newly created County of Washington, comprising that part of the District of Columbia east of the Potomac River that lay outside Georgetown and the City of Washington. He sat on that court for the next four years.

The new house that had been built with such hopes for the future soon became a sad one, for Ann Dorsey's health began to fail in 1802. She went for a change of climate to the hills of Maryland, but without success, for she died in November, leaving her husband with five children, the youngest of whom was only two years old. To add to his troubles, Dorsey's real estate ventures were catching up with him. Heavily indebted to the widow of David Burnes and her son-in-law, General John Peter Van Ness, Dorsey was forced to mortgage the Rock of Dumbarton, "the tenement upon which the said Dorsey now resides containing 22 acres of land." Two bonds dated 27 April 1802 and totalling $10,562 plus interest were to become due in April 1809.

To ease his problems, Dorsey was obliged to sell to Peter Casanove the property at Fair Hill that he had inherited from his wife, but as the buyer died before the deal could be completed, Dorsey sold the place at auction in 1803 for £1350, keeping only the quarter-acre family burying ground where he had presumably laid his wife so recently. These expedients, however grave, were insufficient to rescue Dorsey from the net of his land speculation, for he was unable to sell or lease enough of his Washington lots to pay for his purchases there. By April 1805 he was obliged to mortgage some of these leases to General Van Ness and, sadder still, to dispose entirely of the Rock of Dumbarton.

Dorsey sold the property to Robert Beverley for $15,000, $11,000 of which was in the form of a mortgage which he turned over to Van Ness. He moved back into Georgetown with his motherless children and with his wife's aunt, Rosetta Lynn, who had lived with the family ever since their early days at Fair Hill. In 1807 he married Rosetta, who was twelve years his senior. Two years later they moved to Baltimore, where he helped settle his father's affairs when Colonel Dorsey died in 1810. The last years of his life were spent at Oakley, near Brookville, Montgomery County, another property which he had inherited from Ann. This log and frame house, still standing today, had somehow escaped the fatal pattern of William Hammond Dorsey's real estate speculations, which continued until his death in 1819.

CHAPTER III

The Virginia Beverleys
at Acrolophos

R OBERT BEVERLEY, who bought William Hammond Dorsey's Rock of Dumbarton on 19 April 1805, did so for family reasons that from the documents are less than crystal-clear. A great-grandson both of Robert Beverley (1673–1722), author of *The Present State of Virginia*, published in 1705, and of William Byrd of Westover, he lived at Blandfield, on the Rappahannock River in Essex County, Virginia, in a house built by his grandfather, William Beverley (1698–1756), who was William Byrd's son-in-law. His father, also Robert (1740–1800), had attended Trinity College, Cambridge, and had married Maria, a daughter of Landon Carter of Sabine Hall, Richmond County, and granddaughter of Robert ("King") Carter. Robert Beverley, born to Robert and Maria Beverley in 1769, had followed his father to Trinity College at the age of seventeen. While in England he was under the wing of his father's old school companion, James Bradshaw. Soon after his return from England, the younger Robert Beverley married Jane Tayloe, a daughter of John Tayloe of Mount Airy, Richmond County, thus becoming a brother-in-law of the John Tayloe who built the Octagon House in Washington and of William Augustine Washington, the President's nephew.

The older Robert Beverley died in 1800. Four years later his widow Maria — seemingly tired of plantation life at Blandfield — entered into an agreement with her son Robert which, dated 21 February 1804, reads in part:

Robert Beverley for and in consideration of the wish expressed by Maria Beverley to live with him in Alexandria or George Town, as the case may be; . . . he the said Robert doth hereby agree . . . to provide a *comfortable and convenient home in Alexandria or George Town* for the accommodation of his mother and his own family. Robert Beverley hereby agrees to furnish a *plentiful table of the best sort of provision* the market may afford, as long as the said Maria Beverley may choose to live with him. Robert Beverley agrees to keep for the benefit of the ladies of his family a *genteel coach with a pair of suitable horses.* To clothe the servants of Maria Beverley in neat and sufficient manner, and to pay the taxes upon Maria Beverley's servants.

In return for this carefully stipulated promise of comfortable support, Maria Beverley turned over to her son

all the property she has a right to dispose of by gift upon the estate called Blandfield, and is also about the house . . . and it is hereby understood that if Maria Beverley shall at any time hereafter choose to leave the family of Robert Beverley, that Maria will hereby be entitled to the use for her life of that part of the furniture given to her son Robert that may be removed to Alexandria.

Equally careful arrangements were made about the Blandfield slaves. Maria was allowed to select 25 Negroes for her service during her life, although they were to remain the property of Robert. She was to take to the new house a "man cook," two house men, and two housemaids. Robert agreed to provide her "annually a quarter cask of good wine, should her consumption of that article amount to as much, during her life," and to furnish her "annually a quarter cask of good peach brandy" if she should leave his household.

In compliance with this agreement, Robert Beverley bought the Rock of Dumbarton from the financially embarrassed William Hammond Dorsey and moved his family there. With memories of his Cambridge Greek in mind, he renamed the tree-covered hill "Acrolophos"! Beverley added to the east of the house the charming structure that is now called the Orangery, a rectangular pavilion with seven tall arched sash windows (18 panes over 18) on each side and three on the end. There are marked similarities between this structure and the side wings of the Orangery at Wye House, Talbot County, Maryland, which was the home of Beverley's brother-in-law, Colonel Edward Lloyd. The slope of the roof and

the details of the cornice are much alike, although at Wye the arched
windows are taller (30 panes over 24) and there is a two-story central
pavilion. No documents indicate the year of construction of the Orangery, but the architectural historian, Professor James Grote Van Derpoel
of Columbia University, inclines to "place it slightly later than the
ascribed 1801 date of the house itself," suggesting a date between 1805
and 1812. He notes that the "masonry construction involves the use of
corner pilasters with a simplified detail suggestive of a regency approach"
and calls attention to the similarities of the Wye House Orangery in
support of a date within Beverley's ownership. After all, William Hammond Dorsey had no obvious tie with Wye House, while the younger
Mrs. Beverley's sister, Elizabeth (Tayloe) Lloyd was its mistress.

Sir Augustus John Foster, Secretary of the British Legation, and later
Minister, whose record of Washington life in the early nineteenth century is lively, wrote that there was "a good deal of dining out" and
included Mr. Beverley among the gentlemen — "all good English
names" — who "feasted us in their turn, or had occasionally very pleasant evening parties. Compared with the society of many an English
provincial town, I confess I thought they were seen to much advantage."
Not as much could be said for the state of the streets in the new capital,
for Foster noted, "In driving to assemblies one had sometimes to drive
three or four miles within the city bounds and very often at great risk
of overturn or of being what was termed 'stalled' or stuck in the mud
when one can neither go backward or forward and either loses one's
shoes or one's patience." But once out of the mud, and at one's destina-
tion, things could be pleasant, for

There is no want of handsome ladies for the balls, especially in Georgetown.
Indeed I never saw prettier girls anywhere. . . . Cards were a great resource
of an evening, and gaming was all the fashion, at Brag especially, for the men
who frequented society were chiefly from Virginia and the western states and
were very fond of this most gambling of all games as being one of countenance
as well as cards. Loo was the innocent diversion of the ladies, who, when they
were looed, pronounced the word in a very mincing manner.

Foster thought well of Robert Beverley's brothers-in-law, who owned
two of the handsomest houses in Washington. Of John Tayloe, of the

Octagon House, he observed that he "would be considered a man of large fortune in any country and . . . gave dinners occasionally to foreigners and members of Congress. He had a very fine place at Mount Airy in Virginia and was formerly a gentleman of the turf, having been educated at Cambridge University when it was still the custom here to send young men to England to school or college." Colonel William Augustine Washington, who had married Mrs. Beverley's sister, Sallie Tayloe, and lived in Kalorama, across Rock Creek from Acrolophos, was described as "a very worthy man . . . but he was a martyr to the gout and I saw but little of him." Mrs. William Thornton, who carefully recorded her drives and calls, would go with Mrs. John Tayloe to Mrs. Beverley's and Mrs. Washington's to play chess.

Acrolophos, although still outside the limits of Georgetown, was becoming less and less secluded. The area to the east, where Oak Hill Cemetery now is, had been sold by Thomas Beall of George as the site for a ropewalk, but by 1810 this clumsy industry had been displaced by a fair ground known as Parrott's Grove, later Parrott's Wood, where the fairs of the Columbian Agricultural Society attracted great crowds. According to the *National Intelligencer* of May 1811, a semiannual exhibition there "was attended, as usual, by several hundred of the most respectable ladies and gentlemen of the District and neighboring counties of Virginia and Maryland, among whom were the President, heads of departments, and generally all the prominent officers of the government, the French minister, and our minister to France." Livestock, wool, and other items of agricultural interest were exhibited at these fairs. In addition the grounds were used for Fourth of July celebrations and other outdoor gatherings involving feeding and oratory.

In the years between his purchase of Acrolophos and the war of 1812, Robert Beverley had business in Georgetown, as well as the family reason of his mother's inclination. In November 1809, when subscription books were opened at the Union Tavern for the new Union Bank, a capital of a million dollars was raised and Beverley was elected President. He resigned that office, however, in 1811, the year the bank was incorporated by Act of Congress. He was also engaged in shipping, which became an increasingly uncertain business with the progress of the Napoleonic wars and Mr. Jefferson's Embargo. In regard to the course that the Madison administration tried to steer between the Scylla of Britain and the Charybdis of France, Robert Beverley's views resembled those of the Federalist shipowners of New England. Being pro-British as a matter of self-interest, besides having been educated in England, he struck up a warm friendship with Francis James Jackson, the controversial British Minister to the United States, who arrived in this country in the summer of 1809. Known as "Copenhagen Jackson" for his high-handed activities in Denmark in 1807, the new Minister energetically undertook to sway American public opinion in a manner that would today render a diplomatic representative immediately unacceptable.

Jackson arrived in Washington on 8 September 1809 with his wife — a Prussian baroness, noted for the smartness of her hairdos, which Dolly Madison is said to have copied — two children, a landau barouche, and liveried coachman and servants, all calculated to impress "the natives." Bringing with them "the outfit of long residence," the Jacksons took over the Peter house (now 2618 K Street, N.W.), which had been occupied by the two previous British Ministers, "a house that stood amid fields overlooking Rock Creek and Georgetown." They bought saddle horses and proceeded to roam the countryside. Henry Adams, who was acid about Jackson's mission in his *History of the United States*, observed that at least he "had the merit to discover that Washington was beautiful." So Jackson himself stated, but with qualifications about the inhabitants, when he wrote, "The country has a beautifully picturesque appearance, and I have nowhere seen finer scenery than is composed by the Potomac and the woods and hills above it; yet it has a wild desolate air from being so scantily and rudely cultivated, and from want of population. The natives trouble themselves little about it; their thoughts are chiefly of tobacco, flour, shingles, and the news of the day."

Jackson got on a great deal better with his Georgetown neighbor Robert Beverley than with the administration to which he was accredited. By November 1809, having been told bluntly that neither President Madison nor his Secretary of State would have further dealings with him, Jackson set out on a tour of the eastern states, intending to influence public opinion in favor of Great Britain as best he could. He moved slowly up the coast, finding more and more congenial friends the nearer he came to Federalist New England. That this progress was reported in detail to Robert Beverley in lengthy letters suggests that Jackson regarded Beverley as a figure of influence in Georgetown and Virginia; otherwise, on so brief an acquaintance, he would hardly have taken the time to write as he did. From Baltimore he wrote:

After all I shall reflect with satisfaction on having known in this Country several estimable Characters whose Good Qualities would be an Ornament to any other in the world . . . Yourself and Mrs. Beverley, and some of your Neighbours to whom my Wife and I had looked forward for many hours of social Enjoyment during the ensuing Winter, will command our sincere regrets. Little as we are known to each other, we reflect with mingled pain and pleasure that a longer Acquaintance would have rendered more sensible the Concern of parting.

That Jackson had been making friends by giving shipowners "passports" that would ensure them from capture by the British fleet is indicated by the following letter from New York on 1 February 1810 to Beverley, who was then fitting out some of his vessels for a voyage. "Send me the names and Tonnage of Ships, Port of Departure, where bound and name of Captains, and I will do what I can, but under the Rose [i.e. *sub rosa*], as you say that it is supposed that I cause to be captured all Vessels not provided with my Passport." Beverley promptly sent the information requested, which was acknowledged by Jackson in a letter of 23 February 1810.

The Frost [i.e. ice] being now gone — and the Restrictions which were laid on my Pen being removed by the sailing of the Packet — it is time to acknowledge your letter of the 5th and to send you the enclosed Pass which I beg you to use only for yourself and to take no further notice of, as I had determined before your letter came to issue no more. My readiness as ever to attend to your Wishes had induced me in this instance to depart from the Determination; as I will also do in the case of the *Allegany* — if you are still thinking of sending her to [?] notwithstanding the news from thence, be so good as to mention her Tonnage, and Cargo, as well as the other particulars.

Jackson had been invited by Christopher Gore, the Federalist Governor of Massachusetts, to visit Boston, and although Gore and his party were turned out of office in the spring elections, he went there in June 1810 and was warmly received by Federalist merchants, if not by Governor

John Brooks, and given a public dinner on the 11th. He then visited Niagara Falls, Montreal, and Quebec, before going to Albany. There he had the unusual experience of seeing himself burned in effigy, and he proceeded to New York, from which he sailed for England in mid-September 1810 in H.M.S. *Venus*, one of the vessels that had bombarded Copenhagen at his behest in 1807. A letter to Beverley from New York shortly before sailing, which indicates that Beverley had helped liquidate Jackson's personal affairs in Washington, concludes with a sentence prophetic of events that have only taken place within the last decade. "I have lately seen a very interesting part of the States — where again the Necessity of good Neighbourhood to our mutual Wants is most evident. — The St. Lawrence may become the channel of our joint Prosperity."

Neither "good Neighbourhood" nor "joint Prosperity" between the United States and Great Britain were to increase within the next few years. The war of 1812 evidently put an end to Robert Beverley's shipping operations, for he promptly returned to Blandfield on its outbreak. Although he continued to own Acrolophos for another decade, he never lived there again. His mother went on preferring Georgetown to Blandfield, but at some point she sought other quarters, for in 1816 she was living in Cherry Street. Various Beverley children, however, stayed at Acrolophos from time to time. The oldest daughter, Maria, settled there after her marriage to Dr. Robert Clarke, just before the war of 1812. Occasionally William Beverley, the oldest son, who was to inherit Blandfield, visited there, as did each of the three younger daughters, Rebecca, Jane, and Roberta. It was, however, the second son, James Bradshaw Beverley, named after his father's old friend and adviser at Cambridge, who was most intimately connected with the place.

In 1809, when William Beverley was ready to enter college, the times were not propitious for continuing the Cambridge tradition of his father and grandfather. Therefore Robert Beverley sent his eldest son to Dickinson College at Carlisle, Pennsylvania, and the next year sent the younger boy, James Bradshaw, to join him. Dickinson College, founded in 1783 and presided over at the time by the Reverend Jeremiah Atwater, a Vermonter who was a Yale graduate, attracted the Virginia and Maryland gentry. An 1811 catalogue shows, in addition to the Beverleys, a Lee, a Mason, two Corbins, a Randolph, a Carter, and a Mackall, as well as other boys from Georgetown and Alexandria, out of a student body of 110. Following graduation, it was decided that William's career was to be in business and James Bradshaw's in the law. Accordingly in 1813 the younger son entered a private law school at Litchfield, Connecticut, that had been founded around the time of the Revolution by Tapping Reeve. Although the school was never formally incorporated, its reputation attracted students from distant states, among them John Caldwell Calhoun from South Carolina.

James Bradshaw's letters from Litchfield to his father are full of concern about the war, the British burning of Washington, and rumors that Blandfield would be threatened by a British advance up the Rappahannock. Obviously Robert Beverley's pocket had been pinched by the war, for James Bradshaw, writing home in the perennial manner of students about expenses, apologizes thus:

That I have spent more than is *absolutely* necessary I allow, but that surplus has been small, and comparatively nothing. . . . The only expenses above the bare necessities of life that I could at this time wish to be allowed (for I have never asked the privilege, neither do I wish it, of gambling, drinking, and frolicking) is a very favourable amusement which the Students and Young Ladies frequently participate in, I mean, sleighing — and with such company as I mentioned — for an assemblage of Gentlemen alone on such occasions would but produce the above effects of drinking, etc.

The son, as good a Federalist as his father, passed along news of the political temper of New England; indeed the Hartford Convention opened its deliberations only thirty miles from Litchfield the day after this letter was sent. An undated letter from father to son, evidently written early in 1815, for it mentions the peace signed at Ghent on 24 December 1814, shows the harassment of war upon Robert Beverley's affairs.

My dear Bradshaw,

Your letter of 25th ultimo I have before me. Among many subjects that have given me lately uneasiness the difficulty of your situation for money was not overlooked. So far removed from any place of business I was not able by any possibility to make a new arrangement for you. Indeed my son the disasters of the war had reduced my finances so low that I often determined to sit down and write you that you would be obliged to leave Litchfield on the score of my inability to make you remittances. I however so deeply lamented the consequences that I postponed deciding. And now the peace blessed as the event is for the country at large has found my salt not sold, by which I lose a large sum of money. This was my own fault but I had reasoned myself into a belief there would be another campaign. So it is, it is one of the hardest rubs of my life, and one too you will all feel for a time.

The last sentences indicate a doubtful future for Acrolophos, for with the abandonment of his commercial ventures there was no point in Robert Beverley's returning to live in Georgetown. But he suggests that Bradshaw might find it a useful base for his future legal practice, and proposes that he live there with his sister and brother-in-law, Dr. Clarke, while continuing to read law.

I have written Mr. English to request him to request Mr. Catlin to remit you in suitable notes one hundred dollars. This my son pray husband for I know not when I can get any more to you. William and myself have talked the matter over and I am desirous you should leave Litchfield in the spring. The precise time you may determine yourself. I have supposed my son it would be better for you to settle in George Town than perhaps any where else. I suppose as the Public buildings are to be rebuilt — the Union will no longer be hazarded, that the district [of Columbia] will be a tolerable situation for you, a man of eminence, as none other will do much anywhere and I own I have flattered myself that this would one day be your standing.

In reference to any property I may have to leave you, your situation in George Town will be best adopted and at any rate in time to come it will be very well however eminent you may be to have a good establishment on this spot. Besides you will then be convenient to some interests you may have by inheritance to attend to in the Upper parts of Virginia. You will be convenient to the higher courts of Maryland, and if very eminent you may get some of the Baltimore business in these higher courts. These seem to be better reasons than any other I can present. There is another, you will live whilst reading law at a much less price and much more comfortable with your sister than you would anywhere else and there will be less money outpouring than in any other way.

So in the spring of 1815 James Bradshaw Beverley returned to live at

Acrolophos with his sister and her husband, while continuing to read law with Francis Scott Key, recent author of "The Star Spangled Banner," whose wife, Mary Tayloe Lloyd, daughter of Edward Lloyd of Wye House, was Bradshaw's first cousin. While attempting to further his career, Bradshaw also had to do what he could to keep Acrolophos in passable repair. On 25 February 1816 he wrote his father about fence posts sent from Blandfield: "On first reading your letter respecting the posts I counted them and find that from the upper gate to the corner of the land there are 50 pannels of pailings and you have sent only 40 posts and I also think that these pannels are longer than the common post and rail pannels. I now discover that you inquired of the whole front fence which I did not count but which I will do and inform you by the next post." If his mind was not clearly focused on fence posts, he had the excuse of having recently fallen in love. The girl was Jane Peter, who lived in Peter's Grove across the street. She was the daughter of the late David Peter and granddaughter of Robert Peter, the first mayor of Georgetown and the builder of the house across Rock Creek in which Francis J. Jackson had briefly lived.

Bradshaw had already given his father some hint of what was going on, and Robert guessed the rest. Then in a letter of 9 July 1816 the nineteen-year-old lover came out in the open to ask his father's consent to his engagement to Jane Peter.

Dear Father,

I now address you on a subject of the utmost importance, and in behalf of myself only. Perhaps you may have anticipated me, and from your last letter I presume you have, which I am very glad of. I should have informed you of it some time since. But I did [not] know that the affair would have taken such a serious turn, which had it not would have been unnecessary. But I am entering upon the argumentative without a narration. I have formed an attachment for Jane Peter, which from a very careful examination of my heart, I think I may pronounce to be lasting. As I have always been a pretty susceptible youth, I have never been without some particular partiality, but I have never felt one before so ardent and pure and one that promised so fairly to be lasting. And now I appeal to you for your opinion of it.

Her family and fortune afford me strong assurances that it will meet with your approbation. But at the same time I assure you that these considerations have not been the cause of the attachment. It is founded upon a congeniality of disposition, and nourished by her amiable qualities. In forming my opinion of her I was obliged necessarily to bestow unusual attention to her, which led the family into a suspicion and at last a knowledge of my object — which they now expect. I understand there is to be an equal division of the property among the children, who are five in number — at all events I have heard a relation of hers estimate her portion at $30,000 — the present value — and the nature of the property is such that it will without doubt be greatly enhanced in value.

This attachment has existed since the middle of the winter.

These are the circumstances which I submit to you. And you may believe them to be true. I know the great importance of the subject too well not to be sincere. It has occupied my thoughts for the last six months. And I am prepared to say it is *necessary* for my happiness.

My only wish at present is to *address* her. I should not desire to be married until I had completed my studies.

Now I beg you answer this letter explicitly and as soon as possible, for my suspense is torturing.

When William comes up I will use all my endeavours in recommending some plan that will meet with both yours and his approbation. . . .

In a concluding reference to his mother's death, which had occurred on 16 May, at the early age of 43, he drily notes:

I thought it was unnecessary to tell you that if I wore mourning, I should have to lay aside my blue suit which is my only one.

Your affectionate son,
J. B. Beverley

This tactful letter produced no result. Although Bradshaw went to Blandfield to discuss the matter, his father brought up objections. Apparently Robert Beverley felt that his earlier ties with the Federalist party would make it difficult for his son to succeed, either in the courts or the politics of the District of Columbia. Robert objected to the age of the pair, and evidently suggested that he should not proceed with his courtship unless he were prepared to give up Acrolophos and move west. Mrs. Peter, when consulted, thought such a course unreasonable and unnecessary, but made it clear that "under more favorable circumstances" she would consent to Bradshaw "proceeding in the affair." Thus on 29 July he wrote an impassioned and lengthy plea to his father, which concluded:

My desires you know are moderate . . . and marriage I should not contemplate within 2½ or three years. And at the same time I will tell you I never should be so blindly attached to George Town or any other place as to remain in it when I find it impossible to succeed. But you will find by your enclosed letter [obviously the one earlier quoted] that not two years ago my prospects in George Town were better than any where else.

Francis Scott Key, Bradshaw reported, was on the point of giving up his practice in the lower courts, retiring to his farm, and continuing only his more important cases before the Supreme Court. Thus Bradshaw would be in the way of inheriting Key's work in the lower courts. Moreover, the Potomac was about to be dredged; Georgetown commerce would expand, and there would indeed be business for lawyers.

Under this barrage, Robert Beverley finally surrendered, but he did not want Bradshaw and his bride to be weighted down by Acrolophos. He proposed its sale, one third of the proceeds going to William, as eldest son and heir to Blandfield, and the other two-thirds to Bradshaw as his patrimony. This was entirely satisfactory to the boy, who wrote his father:

The share alloted me is as much as I could ask, it is as much as I could desire. If you recollect when you spoke of selling Acrolophos I disapproved of it, but I was then under the impression and *expectation* that it would be the residence of the family, but since that question is definitely settled, my opinion is different. For in it there is a large capital employed, for which there is no capital accruing — and moreover the decay of the place is very considerable, and unless repaired will continue to be very rapid; which will keep down any increase in the value of the property.

This was all good sense. Acrolophos was not self-sufficient, nor big enough to farm with slave labor. It was a handsome suburban property that would produce only outgo rather than income.

The price of $30,000 that Robert Beverley placed upon Acrolophos — twice what he had paid for it — seemed likely to frustrate the sensible plan of selling it. Bradshaw, on 15 October 1816, thus warned his father:

We have patiently and continuously enquired of all judges the value of property, and of Acrolophos — and find none, except those who immediately join it, who estimate at 30,000 — and I fear you have overated it, and that the sum cannot be got. I wish you distinctly to state is that the least sum that you will agree to take, and if not then to fix your price. William concurs in this. I am anxious that some measures should be taken. The house looking as it does and no one living in it this winter the walls will certainly suffer very much and the inclosures certainly cannot stand through the winter. If you will mention the least sum, then we can offer and get as much as possible.

Plans were made for an auction, at which friendly agents bidding for the owner would prevent a sale below $30,000. At this point a Mr. Plater — possibly a relation, for Bradshaw's maternal grandmother was Rebecca Plater — appeared as a prospective buyer. Bradshaw sent his father the good news on 28 November.

Mr. Plater wrote a note to me two days ago relative to the Sale of Acrolophos upon which I went to him and told him the price distinctly to be $30,000 and any part of the property would be in proportion to this price. He wishes to buy the house and so much of the ground as runs from the eastern line to about 40 feet west of the house. He told me to write you he wished to buy the place for his residence and not for any speculating purpose and therefore he wishes you to put the lowest price. I replyed that the price was fixed and that it was immaterial to you whether the object of the purchase was speculation or otherwise. He wishes you to make a particular valuation, i. e. state the price of the house, and also of the ground per acre, that if he buys he may know what he is about. I wish you therefore in your next to make a valuation per acre and of the house that I may inform him.

Robert Beverley would not budge a dollar; hence no sale. On 16 December, Bradshaw wrote again describing a plan to divide undeveloped land into building lots.

Mr. Plater has declined any further consideration of the subject of the purchase of Acrolophos — he says the price is far above what he thinks the value, and therefore declines making an offer. I have published the advertisement, and appointed Tuesday the 14th of January for the day of the Sale — and filled up the blank acres with nine or ten, for I think ten will about extend 40 feet west of the house — it will be necessary I think to have it surveyed, and if you think so I wish you would direct it in your next. If ten acres be fixed upon to go with the house, the residence according to your last valuation per acre will amount to $8,000; and then leave the price of the house with the proposed ground at $21,200.

The spectacle of a nineteen-year-old boy being left to handle the affair by himself makes one wonder how seriously Robert Beverley really anticipated a sale. He had certainly placed a discouraging price on the property. At this point Dr. and Mrs. Clarke moved from Acrolophos to Gay Street in Georgetown, "borrowing" the dining room carpets, and leaving a slave named Charles as caretaker. Where Bradshaw lived at this juncture is not clear, but he "moved the wine because of the Robberies committed in Town" — altogether fourteen demijohns and 267 bottles. He further reported that the tax collector had presented a bill of $43.27 for Robert Beverley's direct tax for 1815 and 1816.

In the *Daily National Intelligencer* of 14 December 1816 the following advertisement appeared:

For Sale

The House, with a Lot containing nine or ten acres of ground, known in Georgetown as the late residence of Robert Beverley, Esq. This situation is on the confines of the town, just without the limits of the Corporation, and is one of the much admired seats on the heights of Georgetown, and perhaps the most rural of any of them. It borders on a retired part of the town, is quite near enough to be convenient to any interests the owner may have to attend to in the town (Georgetown) or in the western part of the City of Washington, and sufficiently far to give him the pleasure and retirement of the country. The House is well built, very spacious and convenient, and very well suited to the accommodation of a large family; a good garden and excellent water, and other usual conveniences. It will be exposed to public sale on the premises, on Tuesday the 14th of January next, at 1 o' clock, P.M. unless it be previously disposed of at private bargain. The title is perfect, and the premises are entirely unencumbered. One-third of the purchase money will be required to be paid on the delivery of the deed, and the remaining two-thirds, with interest thereon, in two years, for which purpose a negotiable note, with an approved endorser, will be required, to be secured by a deed of trust on the property.

J. B. Beverley

Georgetown, Dec. 14

As the day approached, Bradshaw was busy with arrangements. The auctioneer reported the need of more than one "bye-bidder" to keep the place from going below the set price. Bradshaw was lining up Uncle John Tayloe, if he got back from Philadelphia in time, and George Peter, "if not engaged in the House of Representatives that day." Of course nothing came of the auction. The property was not sold, for Robert Beverley's reserve price of $30,000 was far too high. As long as he stuck to it, the house wasn't likely to sell, which boded no good to Bradshaw Beverley and Jane Peter. Moreover the economic scene was constantly darkening.

Acrolophos seemed to have been left in Bradshaw Beverley's lap. His father and brother at Blandfield seemed quite untroubled by what did, or did not, happen in Georgetown. A year and a quarter later, Bradshaw offered a tenant, writing thus to his father on 1 April 1818: "I am desired by Mr. Burnet to know whether you will rent Acrolophos for five or six months commencing now — and if so to know your price. I think it is highly necessary to leave the place repaired and rented particularly to have it painted — for I do not believe any person will rent it as it is and altho' painting will cost money yet the rent will more than repay it." Seemingly Mr. Burnet did not rent the house, nor was it painted, but on 24 April a county tax bill of $34.50 and the auction advertisement fee of $13 were submitted. Through all this dreary period, Bradshaw persisted in his suit. With his marriage set for the spring of 1819, he apparently convinced his father that he and Jane could swing Acrolophos if his father would give some support. Thus on 28 September 1818, he reported on the progress of repairs: "The outside of Acrolophos is finished, except for the painting which will be done now in a day or two — but I think it better to go on at once with the painting inside, for you do not know that in winter it cannot be done — the repair of the outhouses, kitchen, steps, etc. should be done immediately. . . . Redman is extremely vexatious for the taxes — he is dunning me whenever he sees me. I have got it reduced to $6.34." In December he wrote his father about the furniture situation; a set of chairs for the drawing room — "I find the old ones very much abused" — a bookcase, and "a sopha and a straw carpet for the dining room" were high on his list of priorities, but a more important question was that of service. "What is your plan about the servants? — hired ones are not to be had and if had cannot be relied on." Obviously slaves from Blandfield were needed. On 23 February 1819 Bradshaw reported that an apparently honest and industrious "Englishman just from England" named Honeywell had applied for work as a gardener, but that they could not agree on terms. "He is very poor and will not engage on shares as I wish and that is the only objection — he wants certain wages — he is a man of family but they are in England." Clearly what was contemplated was a revenue-producing fruit and vegetable garden in which the owner supplied the land, the gardener did the work, and both shared in the proceeds, but this did not pan out, for on 9 March Bradshaw again reported to Blandfield, "I cannot get a gardener — none will undertake it in its present condition on the shares. Is one of the boys that you propose for me able to work a garden?" To add to his troubles, his wardrobe was obviously in no state for a wedding, as he remarked: "My shirts are very much wasted — have you linen cambrick to ruffle them?" By 9 April, his marriage was definitely fixed for the 29th of the month, a pump had been put in and the outhouses repaired, but there were matters still to be settled inside the house. "I am now about ascertaining the relative cost of papering and painting the dining room — the latter I suspect is cheapest, unless we use the most common paper, particularly as the wall has been painted before."

In the end the wedding took place, not on 29 April but on 6 May 1819, at Peter's Grove, with the Reverend Mr. Addison performing the ceremony. The young couple moved into a makeshift Acrolophos — a decaying house with scanty furniture, run-down grounds and gardens, and precious little money to keep the place up. Bradshaw Beverley was doing all he could to build up his law practice, but without much success, for 1819 was a year of national economic depression. After nearly a year of marriage things were far from bright, as he informed his father on 20 April 1820.

As I have not heard from you relative to the request I made of a cook I presume there is no one which you can spare and recommend. And if so, we must do as well as we can with the one we have tho' it is at much inconvenience and vexation. With Kisiah we are very well satisfied — she has been somewhat careless in breaking things, but that is her greatest fault as yet. Dick is very useful — and is getting along with the garden tolerably well — but he could do much more work I am sure. He requires watching.

The times are deplorable — and there is no chance of there [sic] getting any better. And but little profesionable business. In these circumstances I am sailing as close to the wind as possible. And as careful of a cent as it was worth a dollar.

I had hoped much from the garden and the fruit this Summer, but the fruit, all of the tree kind is totally destroyed.

I wish very much for a division of Acrolophos, and would like if you would suggest such a one as thought equal. A sale — at any price, is impossible — I would consent at this time to take $15,000 for my portion — and most gladly — and I would immediately invest it in lands. It is now the only safe property in this country.

Three years before, Bradshaw Beverley had told his father that he "never should be so blindly attached to George Town or any other place as to remain in it when I find it impossible to succeed." The depression of 1819 confirmed this resolve; after fair trial he wanted to leave both Georgetown and the law and buy a farm, for in December of that year he wrote, "I myself desire this occupation above all others and if it be possible to procure a farm I am resolved on it. I have a great fancy for combining farming and politics." But it was easier said than done, for in the autumn of 1820 he was still at Acrolophos, trying conscientiously to make a go of the law, but being obliged to admit: "I have every reason to think that my whole income this present year will not be more than $50. Our Court is not three weeks distant and yet I have not bro't one single suit. Nor have I been absent from my office one day except while at Blandfield and on your business. Besides the impossibility of my ever getting into business here, I think that the professional business is rapidly declining in this Court." With this in mind, he reverted to the thought of selling Acrolophos, which alone could provide the money he needed to buy a farm. But the place had decayed even further since he and Jane had moved into it, and was proving a constant worry and expense. On 2 October 1821 he wrote, "I would seriously advise that Acrolophos be sold — there is not a room upstairs that does not leak — in the passage above it leaks so much and the wall is so damp that a black mould is forming on it, in places the plaster is falling — I do not believe that more than $10,000 will be got for it."

With Acrolophos in this state, Bradshaw Beverley took his pregnant wife to Blandfield for Christmas. They had hoped to travel by steamboat, thus avoiding the long jolting of the stagecoach, but with sudden freezing of the river the steamboat suspended service for the winter. Thus the couple drove to Fredericksburg in a hired hack, where a carriage from Blandfield met them. Evidently there were no law cases to deal with, for Bradshaw and Jane Beverley extended the holidays until the middle of March 1822. During this visit Robert Beverley decided to turn Acrolophos over to his son as an inheritance, whose sale might furnish the means of leaving the law, for on 5 March 1822 he deeded the property to Bradshaw, the considerations being "natural love and affection" and "Five dollars, current money."

When Bradshaw returned to Acrolophos for the first time as owner he found it "in a dreadful state all the fences gone" and plaster falling. Early in April he was cutting locust posts and rails to replace the fences, but the interior was in a parlous state. "The roof of the house leaks not in one place but all over. . . . The Spouts have worn out [so] that they will not carry off the water, which runs down on the sides of the wall, keeps them always damp and that has occasioned the plastering to fall in many places in the front passage — and that which has always been the principal leak in the house has been latterly so bad that all the plastering in its neighborhood has fallen." Early the following July there was a ray of hope, for the first genuine opportunity to sell the property arose. On the 15th Bradshaw wrote: "I have been offered for Acrolophos $7500 cash," with the gloomy commentary "I think this town is done. The empty houses are more than I ever saw in any place in my life." In the excitement of a prospective sale, he had almost forgotten another important piece of news, for he continued, without a break in the letter: "On the 5th of July Jane gave birth to a son, which is a very fine child (they are both pretty well)."

The sale was not only consummated, but turned out to be more profitable than had been originally anticipated, for on 19 August 1822, Bradshaw relayed good news to his father: "I have sold Acrolophos for 10,000 cash or equally as good as cash. 5000 when I give possession and the balance on the 1st Oct. next. I propose to give possession in November — the purchaser is the mother-in-law of the Secretary of War — her name is Colhoun. And there is almost universal opinion that I have made a very good sale. Mr. Plater particularly thinks it a *great sale*." On 27 November 1822 the final contract was completed, with James Edward Calhoun, a naval officer and brother-in-law of the Secretary of War as the nominal purchaser. When $8,700 in cash had been paid and James E. Calhoun's note for the remainder of the purchase price had been received, a deed was signed on 1 April 1823 by which Acrolophos passed from the Virginians who had owned it for twenty years to a distinguished family of South Carolina rice planters and public servants.

Thus Bradshaw Beverley secured the means to buy a property called Avenel in Fauquier County, Virginia, where he was able to farm happily. On 29 October 1822 he wrote his last letter from Acrolophos to his father: "We leave the house in 2 or 3 days. I have been busy packing all morning." But his satisfaction in having made a good bargain was overshadowed by sudden family tragedy. His sisters, Rebecca and Jane, who had contracted fever during an epidemic, were moved to Blandfield. Their brother-in-law, Dr. Robert Clarke, who accompanied them from Georgetown, caught the infection and in a few days all three died. Margaret Bayard Smith reported the triple tragedy in a letter of 12 October 1822: "Dr. Clarke, of Georgetown, he is dead, and the two young and lovely Miss Beverleys, the sisters of his wife. In the course of ten days, all three from youth and health and happiness were torn." Dr. Clarke's wife, Maria, soon followed her sisters and husband to the grave. The older brother, William Beverley, amassed a considerable fortune and inherited Blandfield upon the death of his father in 1843, but as he never married, that property eventually reverted to the son of Jane and James Bradshaw Beverley, who was born in the decaying Acrolophos during the last months that the place remained in the family.

After following Bradshaw Beverley and his wife through so many vicissitudes, I wish I knew what they looked like, but not even my ever-helpful friend, John Melville Jennings, Director of the Virginia Historical Society, can produce their portraits. He tells me that the Beverley family maintains that the Blandfield portraits were seized by Federal troops during the Civil War and transported via gunboat to Baltimore, at which point they disappeared. Be that as it may, the fact that there is not a single portrait of early vintage at Blandfield today, although much superb eighteenth-century furniture and a fine library of eighteenth- and early nineteenth-century books survive on the premises, indicates that something drastic must have happened to cause the portraits to disappear completely.

CHAPTER IV

The Home of John C. Calhoun, Secretary of War

ALTHOUGH the deed to Acrolophos was registered in the name of James Edward Calhoun, the actual purchaser was his mother, the widow of John Ewing Colhoun, a Senator from South Carolina, who had died in 1802. This lady, born Floride Bonneau, came from a Huguenot family who owned a rice plantation on the Cooper River. After her husband's death, she fell into the habit, popular among the Charleston rice grandees, of summering in Newport, Rhode Island, with her sons John Ewing and James Edward and her daughter Floride.

The family were Scots, who could never decide whether their name should be spelled Colquohoun, Colhoun, or Calhoun. Hailing from the vicinity of the Rock of Dumbarton, north of the Clyde, they had migrated to Pennsylvania, and then southward, through Virginia to South Carolina. The most distinguished of the tribe, John Caldwell Calhoun (whose spelling of the name eventually became standard), born in 1782, was the son of Patrick, a cousin of John Ewing. Sent north for his education, John C. Calhoun was graduated from Yale in 1804 and spent a subsequent year at the law school in Litchfield, Connecticut, that James Bradshaw Beverley was to attend a few years later. While a student in New England he saw a good deal of his cousin Floride, the widow of John E. Colhoun, and her family at Newport. His father having died in 1796, and his mother in 1801 before he entered Yale, the young law student deeply appreciated the kindness of this warm-hearted cousin, who made him a part of her own family. His feeling towards her is clearly stated in a letter of 12 August 1805 from Litchfield to Newport:

I thank you much for your affectionate mode of address, which I assure you, is much more agreeable to my feeling than any other. Your whole actions in kindness and affection have been to me, like a mother's tenderness. I know not how, I shall make sufficient returns, unless it be by acting in a manner worthy of your friendship and esteem, which, with the assistance of him who is the author of all good resolutions and actions, I hope to do.

During the summer of 1806 John C. Calhoun still regarded his cousin's fourteen-year-old daughter and namesake, Floride, as one of "the children." Apparently he did not see the girl again until the spring of 1808, when she was sixteen, but that sight sealed his fate. A year later, when he was on the way to success in his profession, her mother's consent to the engagement was secured, although they were not married until 8 January 1811, two months before he went to Washington for his first term in the House of Representatives. During his years as a Representative, he lived in a boarding house when in Washington, as many congressmen of the day did, leaving his family in Charleston. But after his appointment as Secretary of War in December 1817 he bought a house at 6th and E Streets, N.W., just north of the present National Gallery of Art, and established his family there.

The elder Mrs. Calhoun, who had by this time abandoned her husband's spelling of the name, enjoyed the company in Washington and often visited her daughter and son-in-law there. Thus on 7 May 1820, John C. Calhoun wrote his brother-in-law, James Edward, "Your mother is residing with us and appears to be very well satisfied. She will not return to Carolina this summer; and I hope she will make up her mind to take up her permanent residence with us." As the summer climate of Washington, then as now, was a trial to a lady accustomed to Newport, Mrs. Calhoun began looking for a summer place above the heat of the city, and thus relieved James Bradshaw Beverley of his problem. In the summer of 1822 John C. Calhoun wrote his other brother-in-law, John Ewing, "Your mother has bought a splendid establishment in Georgetown at $10,000. The finance is low, but, as she has no need of it, I fear she will in the long run find it dear." It was indeed a good bargain, for the price was $20,000 less than Robert Beverley had asked, and only $2,500 more than his son had a short time before thought was all he could get.

James Edward Calhoun, in whose name the property was deeded, was a young bachelor of comfortable means, who had been appointed a midshipman in the United States Navy in 1816. After serving in the U.S.S. *Congress* during two cruises in Brazilian waters and one to China, he was back in Washington in time to complete the papers concerning the purchase of Acrolophos. On 23 April 1823 the Secretary of the Navy granted him an eight-month furlough. Thereupon his brother-in-law, the Secretary of War, appointed him aide to the engineer Stephen Harriman Long, on an expedition to explore the boundary of the United States in northern Minnesota. J. E. Calhoun soon went off to join the expedition, carrying letters from the British Minister recommending this party of scientists and soldiers to officials on the Canadian frontier. Once James was on his way to follow the Minnesota River to its source and then go northward along the Red River and eastward across Canada to Lake Superior, his mother, sister, and brother-in-law moved to the new house above Georgetown.

They were established there at least by 10 July 1823 when John C. Calhoun's old friend, Brigadier-General Joseph Gardner Swift, the distinguished engineer, reported, "I went to Washington to confer with Mr. Calhoun and Virgil Maxey, Esq.; carried with me for him [Mr. Calhoun], and set out in his gardens, the first Isabella grape of Washington; the next was W. W. Seaton's. The plant flourished there exceedingly well, and grew forty feet the first year."

Calhoun enjoyed the change of air, and on 7 August wrote his traveling brother-in-law, who had then reached Chicago: "We are on the heights of Georgetown, and find the residence delightful. The health of the children is very much improved by the fine air and the abundant exercise in the Grove." Delightful as the new home was in the summer, the state of the roads in winter would have made matters difficult for a man whose official duties required constant appearance in Washington. Thus in the autumn, Calhoun rented the house and returned to his own at 6th and E Streets. On 28 September 1823 he wrote to John Ewing Calhoun, "We have been residing on the heights of Georgetown, which is certainly very healthy and pleasant. I have succeeded in renting James's place at $600, which gives legal interest. We have not heard from him for a long time, but his return may now be expected in a few weeks."

When Brigadier-General Swift had brought Calhoun the Isabella grapevine, he had agreed to write a pamphlet supporting him for the Presidency. This was in due course published under the title *Principles not Men*. Other strong friends supported Calhoun in this, his greatest ambition. It seemed a possibility, for with the Federalist Party dead there was, during President Monroe's second term, a free-for-all scramble for the succession. William H. Crawford was the chief candidate of the states-rights school; Calhoun, John Quincy Adams, and Henry Clay were in competition for the leadership of the nationalists, while Andrew Jackson was the candidate of those most concerned with popular power. The death of William Lowndes of South Carolina in 1822 had eliminated a potential challenge to Calhoun's hopes in his own state. But when the caucuses met early in 1824, Calhoun was not a favorite for the top post, but had to content himself with the second, the Vice Presidency. The blow was hard to take. Mrs. Samuel Harrison Smith, wife of the editor of the *National Intelligencer*, wrote on 11 April 1824, "Mr. Calhoun has removed to his house on the hills behind Georgetown and will live I suspect quite retired the rest of the session. He does not look well and feels very deeply the disappointment of his ambition." John Quincy Adams, the Secretary of State, related that when the Secretary of War missed an important Cabinet meeting a few days later, the Secretary of the Navy went to Georgetown to consult him. "Mr. Southard went over to Georgetown to consult Mr. Calhoun, who was detained at home by his wife's confinement. . . . In about an hour Southard returned from Calhoun's: while he was there with Calhoun, Mrs. Calhoun had a daughter born." The daughter was Martha Cornelia, the first of two Calhoun children born in the house on Georgetown Heights. In May of that year, Calhoun entertained the great Yale scholar, Benjamin Silliman, who wrote of his visit: "We were just in time to see both Houses of Congress in session. We dined with J. C. Calhoun, a distinguished graduate of Yale College who was Secretary of War, and who received us with great cordiality."

As Secretary of War, John C. Calhoun was official host to the Marquis de Lafayette during the Revolutionary general's triumphant return visit to the United States. En route to Washington in October 1824, Lafayette was greeted at Baltimore by an official Army escort, including Major

Christopher Van Deventer, Calhoun's Chief Clerk in the War Department. General Washington's tent, lent by his step-grandson, George Washington Parke Custis, was brought to Baltimore for the occasion. Arriving in Washington on the 12th, Lafayette went to Georgetown to dine at Tudor Place as the guest of Martha Parke Custis Peter, whom he fondly remembered as a little girl at Mount Vernon during the Revolution.

Two days later Lafayette returned to Georgetown. The War Department made elaborate preparation for honoring him, and the *Washington Gazette* reported that "The military made a fine martial display." Captain Randolph's Riflemen, Captain Jewell's Riflemen, Captain Kurg's Artillery, Major Andrews' Cavalry, Captain Corcoran's Light Infantry, Captain Dyer's Riflemen, and Captain L. Beall's Light Infantry made a conspicuous showing. Lafayette's visit even revived the dormant local militia who "came out in solemn column, with music playing and colours flying."

General Lafayette was addressed by James Dunlop and Thomas Corcoran at the entrance to Georgetown. His party was then conducted to the house of the Mayor, to Georgetown College, and to General Walter Smith's. The final stopping-place in this great Georgetown festivity was, according to the *Washington Gazette*, "Mr. Secretary Calhoun's where he was handsomely entertained, and introduced by the Mayor and Gen. Smith to a number of ladies and gentlemen." At four in the afternoon Lafayette returned to the city and an evening engagement at the White House.

After six days of Washington entertainment, General Lafayette, escorted by Secretary Calhoun, visited Alexandria, Mount Vernon, Yorktown, Williamsburg, and Norfolk. A typical newspaper report of the time noted:

The solemn and imposing scene of the visit of Lafayette to the tomb of Washington took place on Sunday the 17th inst. about one o' clock. The General left the steam boat *Petersburg* at anchor off Mount Vernon and was received into a barge manned and steered by Captains of vessels from Alexandria who had handsomely volunteered their services for this interesting occasion. He was accompanied in the barge by his family and suite and Mr. Secretary Calhoun.

Calhoun who was present at the dinners, balls, and other entertainments offered the General, was quick to make appropriate toasts when called upon, and faithfully reported to President Monroe details of the activities. After the Williamsburg reception, for example, he wrote the President: "On his part General La Fayette acquitted himself remarkable well. His replies were all appropriate, and his toasts, tho' evidently unpremeditated, were such as to strike forcibly." Upon returning to Washington from his tour, Calhoun closed the Georgetown house and returned to 6th and E Streets, where he soon entertained General Lafayette, in company with Presidential candidate John Quincy Adams and others.

On 12 November 1824 Calhoun wrote his mother-in-law about the Georgetown house, "I have not yet rented the House, nor sold the carriage and horses. I fear I will find it difficult to do either to advantage. We are now in the city and the House is shut up and is without a tenant. Should I not succeed in getting one, I will get Mr. Smith to take charge of the premises." Then, turning to politics, he continued, "From present appearances your candidate General Jackson will be elected. He is, as far as the returns have come in, far ahead. There seems to be no doubt about my election as Vice President. It will at least have one advantage, that of permitting me to devote more of my time to my private affairs." Calhoun's prediction about Andrew Jackson was incorrect, for the election was thrown into the House of Representatives, which gave the Presidency to John Quincy Adams. Calhoun, who had the curious distinction of running for Vice President on the tickets of both these candidates, was elected without question and took office in March 1825.

In the same month he sold his Washington house at 6th and E Streets to his successor as Secretary of War, James Barbour, for $9,000, exactly the price he had paid for it seven years before, and took off to South Carolina for the summer. Regarding the office of Vice President as a more leisurely one than the Secretaryship of War, he decided to spend the winter at his mother-in-law's house on Georgetown Heights. Thus on 22 September 1825 he wrote from Pendleton, South Carolina, to his former associate in the War Department, Christopher Van Deventer: "You may expect us there between the 15th–20th Nov. We will occupy Oakly this winter."

Previously Calhoun had referred to the Georgetown property rather vaguely as the "House," never continuing the mouth-filling Beverley name of Acrolophos. Now that he was to make it his principal residence, it needed a name, and he gave it the simple and appropriate one of Oakly. There the Calhouns lived during the first session of the 19th Congress, December 1825 to May 1826. Previously Calhoun had signed his letters from Georgetown Heights "Washington"; now he used "Georgetown," although in point of fact at the time Oakly lay outside the limits of both Georgetown and Washington. In April 1826 a son was born there to Mrs. Calhoun, who named him James Edward, after her brother, the legal owner of the place.

Life at Oakly proved so expensive that Calhoun within the year felt obliged to give up living there. He could not, he confessed to his brother-in-law, John Ewing Calhoun, on 14 June 1826, keep the place up on his salary as Vice President and his other income: "The great fall in the price of staple commodity and the impossibility of reducing our expenses consistently with what is due the office I occupy, to the limits of the salary affixed by law, have induced me to change our arrangement of fixing our residence here, instead of the South." For years Calhoun had wished to establish his household permanently in South Carolina, and now at last he decided to move to Pendleton. In informing his mother-in-law of this plan, he wrote, "I will sell this place if a good price offers and you do not object. If not, or if it should not be agreeable to you to sell, I will rent on the best terms we can." They had planned to leave Oakly in the autumn but, because of the serious illness of their son John, did so earlier on 19 July 1826.

John C. Calhoun, who had sold his town house to his successor as Secretary of War, rented Oakly to another official friend and colleague, Major Christopher Van Deventer, an alumnus of Williams College and one of the earliest graduates of West Point, who had served with distinction in the War of 1812. He had been aide-de-camp to Calhoun's friend, Brigadier-General Joseph G. Swift, and had served as Deputy Quartermaster-General. The relationship between Calhoun and Van Deventer had been a close one ever since the former's appointment as Secretary of War in 1817 when he asked Van Deventer to become his Chief Clerk. As General Winfield Scott and William H. Winder shared Calhoun's high opinion of him, it seemed likely that he might long remain in Oakly, of which he took possession as a tenant in July 1826.

In consequence, however, of some political involvement early the next year, Major Van Deventer received on 18 February 1827 a curt note from Secretary Barbour informing him: "Your services as Chief Clerk of the War Department are henceforth dispensed with." Calhoun soon received a letter from his old friend, Virgil Maxey, urging that action be taken to aid this victim of War Department politics:

I understand, however, that a contemptible effort is made to rob you of the credit of the reforms which you effected in the War Department. Van Deventer, who has been made a victim of the malice of your enemies for the sole purpose of making the impression that you had been negligent of your duty in not dismissing him from office, was the first who laid before you a project of the Central Staff. I feel a strong sympathy for Van Deventer, who, tho' strong in conscious integrity, must nevertheless feel a deep mortification at the impression that his abrupt dismissal from office is calculated to make on the public mind.

However unfair or prejudiced Van Deventer's dismissal may have been, he was soon forced to leave Oakly and move to Buffalo to improve his fortunes in business. When eventually he left Buffalo he returned not to Oakly but to Washington, where he died on 22 April 1838 at the age of 49.

With Van Deventer gone, Calhoun found no tenant willing to rent Oakly on satisfactory terms. The following year, he had an opportunity to sell and so wrote his brother-in-law, James Edward, on 23 January 1828, "I have in the last few days made a conditional sale of Oakly for $8,000, subject to the ratification of your mother, which I hope she will confirm. The property is going to waste, with, I think, no prospect of a rise, and the interest on the sum exceeds the rent. It will free her from all her engagements and leave her $2000, or $3000 of disposable funds."

Following the Stephen Long expedition, James Edward Calhoun had made a cruise in the Mediterranean in the frigate *Constitution*. After his commissioning as lieutenant in 1826, he served in Brazilian waters in *Macedonia* and *Boston* and returned to the United States in July 1829, when he was granted leave until further orders. On 5 August 1829 he sold Oakly — still described in the deed as Acrolophos — to Brooke Mackall of Georgetown for $8,000, the price quoted by John C. Calhoun the previous year. He then went to Millwood, near Terryville, Abbeville County, South Carolina, where he had a plantation, whose management he enjoyed so much that in 1833 he resigned from the Navy. In 1839 he married Maria Edgeworth Snokins, who died childless a few years later. He continued to manage the plantation until his death in 1889 at the age of 90.

John C. Calhoun, as everyone knows, was re-elected Vice President on the Jackson ticket in 1828, served in the Senate from 1832 to 1843, was Secretary of State in 1844–45, returned to the Senate in 1845 and continued there until his death in 1850. But that is beyond his connection with Oakly, or Dumbarton Oaks, which came to an end in July 1826.

CHAPTER V

The Ups and Downs of Ninety Years

WHEN James E. Calhoun sold Oakly in 1829, the house had been through a variety of vicissitudes unusual for a handsome place under thirty years old. Dorsey, its builder, enjoyed it for less than four years before his Washington real estate speculations caught up with him. Then for seven years the Virginia Beverleys maintained it properly, and for ten more struggled to keep the roof tight and prevent the plaster from falling. With the South Carolina Calhouns, it changed from an asset to a liability in only six years; moreover they had never regarded it as anything more than a cool summer house, to be rented in winters if possible. For the next forty years the place was to be the year-round home of two very different permanent residents of Georgetown — a customs officer and a retail hardware dealer.

The former of these, Brooke Mackall, had grown up in the town. His father, Leonard Mackall, a son of Benjamin Mackall, a tobacco planter of Prince Georges County, Maryland, had come to Georgetown to engage in shipping and had there married Catherine, a daughter of Brooke Beall. Early in the nineteenth century they had built a house far north in Georgetown, on Road (now R) Street. As a young man Brooke Mackall worked in his father's shipping office, the Georgetown Bank of Columbia, and the Georgetown office of the War Department, and in 1826 he was nominated as Inspector of the Georgetown Customs office.

When Brooke Mackall bought Oakly in 1829 he was still a bachelor, without, it appears, immediate prospects of marriage. Seemingly he was taking advantage of a good bargain, close to his childhood home. The area between the present Que and R Streets, east of Wisconsin Avenue, which formed the chief part of Beall's Second Addition, had become a region of handsome houses set in ample suburban grounds. In the second square east of High Street (Wisconsin Avenue) stood Tudor Place, which still retains its commanding position above Que Street. Then to the eastward came in succession the house of Elisha O. Williams, Peter's Grove, George Washington Corbin's Dumbarton, Mackall Square, Samuel Davidson's Evermay, and Bellevue (renamed in the present century Dumbarton House). Two of Brooke Beall's daughters (and Brooke Mackall's aunts) lived in the region — Harriet, who had married Elisha O. Williams, and Christiana, who with her husband Benjamin Mackall (brother of Leonard and consequently own uncle of Brooke Mackall) had built Mackall Square. Thus the new owner of Oakly not only had agreeable surroundings but was in the midst of his relatives.

In 1834 Brooke Mackall married Martha Jane Simpson, thirteen years younger than himself, who was the daughter of Michael T. Simpson of Bellefonte, Pennsylvania, a veteran of the War of 1812 who held the unexciting post of Superintendent of the Dead Letter Office in the Post Office Department. The couple had a large number of children, at least five of whom were born in the house. It is not clear how a minor government official was able to keep up a place that John C. Calhoun had found too expensive even for a Vice President of the United States. Although the incompleteness of early Treasury Department records makes it difficult to verify the exact nature of Brooke Mackall's progress in the Customs service, it has been stated that President John Quincy Adams appointed him Surveyor of the Port of Georgetown, and that he discharged the greater part of the duties of Collector of the Port without achieving appointment to that office, for which he applied under several administrations. With the turnover in Federal jobs that prevailed under the spoils system, Brooke Mackall eventually lost his Customs post, such as it was, and had to make do with a lesser appointment in the office of the Second Auditor of the Treasury Department.

Upon the death of his father in 1843, Brooke Mackall's financial position further deteriorated, and in 1846 he was forced to sell the house in which he had lived pleasantly for seventeen years. Although the times were poor for real estate, as the Chesapeake and Ohio Canal, which was expected to bring new prosperity to Georgetown, was still unfinished, Mackall got $11,500 for the property, which was $3,500 more than he had paid for it in 1829. He continued to live in Washington, in and out of Federal service, until he died in 1880 in his eightieth year. Brooke Mackall and members of his family were the first occupants of the house to be buried in Oak Hill Cemetery, the beautiful hillside sloping from R Street down to Rock Creek, that William Wilson Corcoran had given to Georgetown in 1849.

The new owner, Edward Magruder Linthicum, who was to remain in possession until his death 23 years later, had a more reliable source of income than Federal employment; he was a successful hardware dealer with a store on the northwest corner of High and Bridge Streets, now Wisconsin Avenue and M Street. Born in 1787 in Montgomery County, Maryland, Linthicum had come to Georgetown about 1819 and gone into the hardware business, at which he prospered. In the mid-thirties he became part-owner of the ships *Caledonia* and *Katharine Jackson*, operated to the West Indies by the Georgetown Exporting and Importing Company, but the retail store that he maintained at the strategic crossroads of Georgetown was the source of his prosperity. By 1846 he had reached the point where he felt it appropriate to exchange his house at 3019 P Street for a handsomer one on the Heights, which would give him space to develop a lifelong fondness for trees and plants. As early as 1825 he had been distributing in his store catalogues of fruit and ornamental trees for the famous nurseryman, Joshua Pierce, whose Linnaean Hill nursery is now part of Rock Creek Park.

The deed by which Brooke Mackall and wife conveyed their house to Edward M. Linthicum on 29 July 1846 described the property as Acrolophos, although there is no evidence as to whether or not the Mackalls used that high-flown name during their occupancy. In his enthusiasm over a significant victory in the war with Mexico, Linthicum renamed the property Monterey, but by 1860 had substituted The Oaks, in tribute to the magnificent white oaks surrounding the house and dominating the landscape, which had first attracted him to the place. Previous owners had been chiefly concerned with keeping the house from falling to pieces. Linthicum, by contrast, greatly enlarged it and radically changed its appearance to make his prosperity clear.

Fortunately the house was photographed about 1860 before these changes were made. Sizeable wings were added on either side; a mansard roof was put on the third floor to gain additional space there, and the main entrance was greatly embellished to accord with the taste of the times. Originally the entrance porch was wooden, with two columns on either side, with a single arched window above on the second floor. Linthicum substituted a larger entrance with wrought-iron decoration. The east wing, which was built first, just before or during the Civil War, contained the dining room, and extended so far to the rear as to transform the ground plan into the shape of a letter L. The west wing, which had no rear extension, was added after the Civil War. At the back of the house in the center an octagonal cupola, of French Second Empire inspiration, was added, rising above the mansard roof, and providing a view over Rock Creek. Along Road (R) Street an impressive stone wall was built surmounted by an iron fence, matching the balustrades of the new porch. Through the substantial stone gateposts of two entrances, a semicircular carriage way led to the front of the house, while to the rear a large brick barn was added. The Orangery, built by Beverley, was repaired and furnished with an up-to-the-minute roof. This was well maintained as a greenhouse, full of plants, including the impressive fig, whose branches still form a labyrinthine pattern on the walls.

William A. Gordon, a Georgetown friend of Linthicum's, wrote of The Oaks in his time:

The house, which has been changed, but not improved in appearance, by the addition of a mansard roof and other alterations, was a large two-story brick, with hall from front to rear "wide enough for a hay wagon to pass through," on either side of which were great parlors beautifully proportioned. The east parlor opened into a bright, sunny dining room, which in turn looked out upon a well-filled greenhouse, with flower gardens on the east, wooded lawn in front, grove of forest trees on the west, and gently sloping well-sodded hills in the rear, all of which were kept in perfect order. During the life of Mr. Linthicum, "The Oaks" was the show place of the District.

It is typical of our tendency to romanticize the past that some later writers on Georgetown history, in quoting this description, substitute a "coach and four" for "hay wagon," as a more elegant unit of measure.

When Linthicum bought the house in 1846, his family consisted only of his wife and an adopted daughter, Kate Mitchell, then nine years old. Shortly before the Civil War Kate was married at The Oaks to Josiah Dent, a Washington lawyer who was almost sixteen years her senior. The enlargement of the house was probably undertaken about this time to provide quarters for the newly married couple, who moved in with the Linthicums. Here their only son, Edward Linthicum Dent, was born on 5 July 1861. When Kate Dent died prematurely on 25 May 1862, the child was adopted by Edward Linthicum. He and his father continued to live at The Oaks.

Edward M. Linthicum died on 30 October 1869, leaving an estate of a quarter of a million dollars. His will, which was replete with the verbiage dear to nineteenth-century self-made men, left a trust fund of $50,000 to establish "a free school for the education and instruction of indigent white boys and youths of said Georgetown in useful learning and in the spirit and practice of Christian virtue," with Josiah Dent as President and William A. Gordon, Jr., and three other friends as Trustees. In a chapter of *A Portrait of Old George Town* entitled "The Three Philanthropists," Grace Dunlop Ecker linked Linthicum's bequests with those of W. W. Corcoran and George Peabody of London, who early in his career had run a dry goods store in Georgetown. Such an association is unduly complimentary, for the Linthicum Institute is hardly to be compared with the Corcoran Gallery or the variety of institutions that owed their origin to George Peabody. Congressman Frederick Stone of Maryland introduced in the 41st Congress a bill (H.R. 1166) to incorporate the Linthicum Institute. Although it passed the House, it was on 6 May 1870 tabled in the Senate. Senator Charles Sumner of Massachusetts was believed to have taken exception to the restrictive segregationist provision of the will, which limited the school to "indigent white boys and youth." In any case such a restriction was illegal, for in March 1869, four months before Linthicum made his will, the word "white" had been eliminated by Federal law from every passage in which it existed in the charter and laws of Washington and Georgetown. The Senate action was the end of Congressional incorporation of the Linthicum Institute.

Henry D. Cooke, the first Governor of the ill-fated and short-lived

Territory of the District of Columbia (1871–74), who wished to build new schools although he lacked the money to pay for them, persuaded the Linthicum Trustees to lend their $50,000 capital toward the construction of the Curtis Public School on P Street, near St. John's Church in Georgetown, which would contain a room for an industrial night school to be managed by the Linthicum Institute. There night classes were offered in penmanship, bookkeeping, mechanical and architectural drawing, geometry, chemistry, physics, and, eventually, typewriting. About 1890, when the loan had been repaid, the Linthicum Institute built quarters of its own at 3116 O Street, N.W., with space for the school on the ground floor and, upstairs, Linthicum Hall, which was considered in the nineties to have the "best floor 'par excellence' for dancing anywhere."

Governor Cooke and his ally in the new territorial government, Alexander ("Boss") Shepherd, bestirred themselves energetically to transform the District of Columbia from its previous status of a series of mudholes to a beautiful city of paved and well drained streets. While their efforts inspired a syndicate of speculatively minded California mine operators to put $600,000 into land near Dupont Circle in 1871, they created less confidence among District taxpayers. The changes in tax valuations on the 22 acres of The Oaks are a case in point. In 1871–72 the land was valued at $17,600 and the buildings at $12,000, and the total tax was $251.60. Three years later, when no major changes had been made in the property, the tax was $1,094.00, for the valuations had been raised to $29,700 on the land and $25,000 on the buildings. When the national panic of 1873 hit, things were in a bad way. Governor Cooke's First National Bank of Washington closed its doors, just as his brother's banking house of Jay Cooke and Company failed in New York. Henry D. Cooke resigned as Governor; President Grant appointed Alexander Shepherd to the post, but as even the assured Shepherd could obtain no credit for the District government anywhere, a Congressional investigation was opened in February 1874. This soon produced evidence of self-seeking and dishonesty that led Congress to abolish the governorship, legislature, and board of public works, placing control of the District temporarily in the hands of three Commissioners to be appointed by the President. Shepherd, although nominated a Commissioner by President Grant, when refused confirmation by the Senate, took off for Mexico, leaving behind him in the disenfranchised city the unfinished mess that he had instigated under guise of civic betterment.

In the course of the Shepherd orgy of construction, Road (R) and other streets in the vicinity of The Oaks were considerably improved by gravel road beds, gas lighting, and the planting of maples. Governor Cooke at one moment even planned a real estate development across the street from The Oaks. Although Josiah Dent had initially worked with Governor Cooke on the construction of the Curtis School, he and many other taxpayers went into opposition when their pockets were affected. Thus in 1876 he joined with W. W. Corcoran and others in the petition to Congress that led on 11 June 1878 to the passage of the Organic Act establishing the present commission form of government for the District of Columbia. On the passage of this act, President Hayes nominated Josiah Dent as one of the three Commissioners, in which capacity he served until 1882.

Josiah Dent was an intimate friend of the Right Reverend William Pinkney, Bishop of Maryland, and the Right Reverend Richard Hooker Wilmer, Bishop of Alabama, who visited The Oaks so frequently that the second story of the west wing came to be called the Bishop's Room. Henry Ridgley Evans, a boyhood friend of Edward Linthicum Dent, who recalled this fact, also remembered, from his visits to The Oaks in the seventies, that the library, on the ground floor of the west wing, was filled with interesting old books, including a first edition of Dr. Johnson's *Dictionary of the English Language* and an early edition of Robert Burton's *Anatomy of Melancholy*. At Christmas, Evans recalled, there was always a huge bowl of eggnog à la Maryland on a Chippendale table in the central hall, and at New Year's a big bowl of apple toddy.

For fifteen years after Edward Linthicum's death, his widow lived at The Oaks with Josiah and Edward Linthicum Dent. On Mrs. Linthicum's death in 1884, the house and the residue of her husband's property passed to the 23-year-old Edward. The 22-acre tract in which The Oaks stood had not changed in size since William Hammond Dorsey bought it from Thomas Beall of George eighty-four years before. It ran along Road Street, then renamed U, and later R Street, from Lover's Lane on the east almost to Wisconsin Avenue on the west, and adjoined the Elverson estate to the north. Like Thomas Beall of George in the previous century, Edward Linthicum Dent, tempted by rising land values, soon began hacking away at his inheritance. He had attended Columbian College, now George Washington University, receiving the degree of Bachelor of Science in 1882 and of Master of Engineering in 1884. He had further borrowed large sums in order to establish the Washington Architectural Iron and Bridge Works and a steam-heating business, and within a few years he was so far beyond his depth in debt that on 26 September 1890 he assigned all his property to William A. Gordon and James H. Taylor as trustees. Thus at various times between 1891 and 1894 the land was sold to meet Dent's obligations.

Two streets were cut into the tract, Observatory Place, named after the Naval Observatory to the north, that is today designated as a part of 32nd Street, and Linthicum Place, now renamed S Street. Observatory Place ran north from Road (or R) Street just west of the house. Linthicum Place ran east from Wisconsin Avenue to meet Observatory Place at right angles at a point that was close to the center of the 22-acre property. The land thus fell roughly into four quarters. The southeast quarter, with the house, was sold to Mr. and Mrs. Henry Fitch Blount, while the southwest quarter was divided into small building lots. The northwest quarter came into the possession of Samuel J. Harriot, trustee, while the northeast quarter was sold in three parts. One of these, a 100-by 300-foot lot just east of the intersection of Observatory Place and Linthicum Place, was bought by Bessie L. Kirbey and became the site of a Home for Incurables that has now disappeared, while the other two were sold to Mr. and Mrs. Blount, thus giving them the rolling hillside behind their house. Thus was the property cannibalized.

The Dent family scattered also, to be rejoined nearby in death. Josiah Dent, when past seventy, had remarried and gone to live in Berkeley Springs, West Virginia. When Edward's business failed, he took a job as a District of Columbia water inspector; then went off with his wife and son to Wilkinsburg, Pennsylvania, where he died, aged 39, on 19 October 1899, a week before the death of his father. They were buried together in the Linthicum tomb in Oak Hill Cemetery, where Edward's widow, Mary, joined them in 1928, and his son Edward Linthicum

Dent, a fifty-year-old Corporal of the 110th Field Artillery, 29th Division, on 10 February 1941.

Henry Fitch Blount, who bought The Oaks and six acres of land from Edward Dent's trustees in September 1891 for $105,000 — nearly ten times what Edward M. Linthicum had paid for the whole 22 acres forty-five years before — was a native of Richmond, Ontario County, New York, who had gone west. Born in 1829 and educated, as he said, "in a little red school house and in my own library," he became a successful manufacturer of ploughs and farm implements at Evansville, Indiana. After the death of his first wife, by whom he had two children, he married in 1864 Lucia Eames of Kalamazoo, Michigan, who became the mother of two sons and two daughters. In 1886 Henry Blount retired from business and took his family abroad for two years in France and Switzerland. On their return to the United States in 1888, the Blounts settled in Washington, where they found congenial means of passing the time. Henry Blount became a Director and, in 1891, a Vice President of the American Security and Trust Company. He joined the Cosmos Club, and was elected to the boards of the Emergency Hospital, the National Reform School, and the National Geographic Society. Mrs. Blount, a charter member of the D. A. R., became for some years its Secretary General. With these interests Washington was a desirable place of retirement; with five children living at home a large house was needed — hence the purchase of The Oaks.

Gradually Henry Fitch Blount was able to reassemble the more attractive parts of the original property from the Dent debacle. A month after his first purchase he obtained for $7,500 a 300 by 100-foot lot to the north. In 1894 he purchased at auction for $16,500 most of the other land in the northeast quarter of the original tract. His three purchases, costing a total of $129,000, represented almost all the eastern half of the land that had been a unit from Dorsey through Linthicum.

The exterior of The Oaks remained much as Edward M. Linthicum had rebuilt it in the sixties, but there were numerous changes within. Instead of the ornate mid-nineteenth-century furniture of the Linthicums, the Blounts installed pieces that they had assembled during their European travels, mostly — to judge by the few surviving photographs — the kind of baronially-suggestive pieces that Continental dealers have long delighted in selling to travelling Americans. There were, for example, a couple of Spanish *fraileros* that the Blounts called their "Ferdinand and Isabella chairs," a credenza with carved portrait medallions of Henry II and Catherine de Medici, carved and tinted ivory medallions of Francis II and Mary Stuart dated 1558, large tapestries, and so on. Such things within, and a pet peacock named Pico on the lawn, gave great pleasure to the new occupants.

The attic of The Oaks was transformed into "The Little Theatre," complete with stage, a "royal box" for distinguished guests, and seats for an audience of two hundred. Sydney R. Burleigh of Providence, Rhode Island, painted wall decorations symbolizing music and the dance, while the pupils of Cavaliere Gaetano Trentanove of Florence made stencils for pseudo-Egyptian wall decorations. The Blount girls had a lovely time planning decorations, raiding other portions of the house for stage sets, and acting in plays that were written by friends of the family. Mabel Hay Barrows, daughter of a Massachusetts congressman, wrote one play; Helen Nicolay, daughter of Lincoln's secretary, wrote another and designed the scenery for it as well. Elizabeth Blount played the principal role in Lawrence Alma-Tameda's "The Silent Voice." There are still elderly people in Washington who remember climbing to the attic of The Oaks for these lighthearted entertainments. And there were gatherings on the lawn as well, like the celebration on 23 May 1910 called the "Daphnephoria," honoring Apollo and the return of the sun, at which the Marine Band for some reason played "The Recessional."

The house was always full of guests, the largest of whom were Queen Liliuokalani of Hawaii, who came to a reception in 1892, and the historian John Fiske, who came whenever he was in Washington on lecture engagements. The Blount children gleefully remembered counting eighteen griddle cakes that Fiske had eaten for breakfast and delighted in the way in which their parents' coupé listed dangerously when weighted down by the historian's bulky person. Alexander Graham Bell, Mr. Blount's closest friend, was a constant visitor. Nicolay and Hay, President Andrew D. White of Cornell, Edward Everett Hale, S. P. Langley, Clara Barton, Susan B. Anthony, Elizabeth Cady Stanton, Julia Ward Howe, Frederick Douglass, President Taft, John D. Long, and

A. R. Spofford, Librarian of Congress, were other guests recalled (more respectfully than John Fiske) by the Blount children.

The Blounts took particular pleasure in planting large clumps of boxwood in the garden. Mrs. Blount would watch the sales of older houses in Georgetown and buy masses of old box from the owners. One that was nearly a hundred feet in circumference gave particular pleasure to the children, who played hide and seek among the labyrinth of its branches.

Henry Fitch Blount died at The Oaks on 10 October 1917 at the age of 88. His wife, who survived him by eight years, continued to live in the house until the autumn of 1920 when she sold it, and the greater part of the land, to Mr. and Mrs. Robert Woods Bliss. Mrs. Blount, who hated to leave the place entirely, then moved to a small building that she had retained in the northern part of the property, which was reached by a right of way through the portion sold. In 1922, however, she parted with this last remnant of the place to Mr. and Mrs. Bliss, who had already begun the complete rebuilding of the house. It had had many names over a hundred and twenty years — Rock of Dumbarton, Acrolophos, Oakly, Monterey, The Oaks. It now became Dumbarton Oaks and entered the most stable and elegant part of its history.

CHAPTER VI

The Creation of
Dumbarton Oaks

THE purchase of Dumbarton Oaks by Mr. and Mrs. Robert Woods Bliss in 1920 was inspired by what he called "a dream during twenty years of professional nomadism of having a country house in the city." In the autumn of 1900, only a few weeks after being graduated from Harvard College, Robert Bliss went to Puerto Rico — then commonly called, in Anglicized spelling, Porto Rico. American military government had been established in October 1898 in that island, which two months later, by the treaty signed at Paris concluding the Spanish-American War, was ceded to the United States. In the civil government created by a Congressional act of 12 April 1900, Robert Bliss served first as a clerk in the office of the Secretary and afterwards, for over two years, as private secretary to Hon. William H. Hunt, the second civil Governor, who proved to be a stimulating and delightful chief. In June 1903 Mr. Bliss entered the Foreign Service of the United States and was assigned as Consul at Venice, where there was then, as he recalled in a Harvard class report, "only one private motor boat to annoy the gondoliers — that of Don Jaime, pretender to the Spanish throne — which puffed about with a huge great Dane standing in the bow." In October 1904 he was sent to St. Petersburg as Second Secretary, where Ambassador George von L. Meyer, who was transferred from Rome to Russia in the spring of 1905, gave the American Embassy an enviable prestige. The next two years in St. Petersburg included part of the Russo-Japanese War and the threatening revolutions that followed it. From there Robert Bliss went to Brussels in January 1907 as Secretary of the Legation, and was in charge during that summer when, after much interesting discussion in the Belgian Parliament, the annexation of the Congo was voted. In April 1908 he was appointed delegate of the United States to the International Conference to consider the revision of the arms and ammunition regulations of the General Acts of Brussels of 2 July 1890.

During his assignment in Brussels, Robert Bliss was married in New York on 14 April 1908 to Mildred Barnes, who was to share in his travels and collecting for the next fifty-four years. The following year they went to Buenos Aires to which he was ordered in August as Secretary of the Legation. They varied the journey to the new post by an overland crossing of the Isthmus of Panama, a trip down the west coast of the continent, and visits to Lima and Santiago, and finally by crossing the Andes on muleback. As the celebrations commemorating the centennial of Argentine independence, which included international expositions, brought distinguished foreigners of all professions to Buenos Aires in 1910, the Legation had a wider sphere of activities than usual in the year and a half that followed, during which Robert Bliss acted continuously as Chargé d'Affaires. This experience proved of value in the next chapter, which began with transfer to Paris as Secretary of the Embassy in February 1912.

On the creation of the grade of Counselor in the Foreign Service in July 1916, Robert Bliss was designated as such at Paris, where he remained in that capacity throughout the war and the Peace Conference, except for the months of September, October, and November 1918, when he was sent to take charge of our Legation at The Hague during the temporary absence of the Minister. Although he deeply regretted that members of the Foreign Service were prohibited from resigning to enter the Army when the United States became a belligerent, the seven and a half years in Paris were crowded with intensive work and responsibility that included intimate association with French, British, Belgian, and other allies, as well as with the American Expeditionary Force. They were also, incidentally, crucial ones in the formation of the collections that were, years later, to find a permanent home at Dumbarton Oaks.

In the preface to *The Robert Woods Bliss Collection, Pre-Columbian Art,* published in 1957, he thus reported the genesis of the collection:

Soon after reaching Paris in the spring of 1912, my friend Royall Tyler took me to a small shop in the Boulevard Raspail to see a group of pre-Columbian objects from Peru. I had just come from the Argentine Republic, where I had never seen anything like these objects, the temptations offered there having been in the form of colonial silver. Within a year, the *antiquaire* of the Boulevard Raspail, Joseph Brummer, showed me an Olmec jadeite figure. That day the collector's microbe took root in — it must be confessed — very fertile soil. Thus, in 1912, were sown the seeds of an incurable malady!

These first objects are the base upon which I have slowly built my collection. . . . As time went on, I would now and again acquire in Europe or in the United States examples of fine workmanship or of an arresting concept. But not one did I ever find in the country of its origin! . . . In a nomadic career spreading over years of close contact with the grindstone of diplomatic life, there were many periods when no temptation came to my door. But always, in lean years or in full, the encouraging enthusiasm and the discrimination of my wife have helped to make this collection what it is.

Many men who succumb to the incurable malady of collecting have to give a clandestine quality to their acquisitions, slipping them into place with the hope that they will not be reproached by their wives. Robert Bliss never suffered from this misfortune, for his wife had contracted the same disease at an early age. While still in her teens in New York she had seen, coveted, and bought a piece of *opus Anglicanum* at a time when such medieval embroideries were little studied or known. As a girl fresh out of school, she was in correspondence with booksellers in Paris, Tours, Clermont-Ferrand, and Rome, seeking precise literary, bibliographical, and artistic information — a habit that remained with her, as one notes from Marcel Proust's letter of 20 May 1918 to Madame Sheikévitch: "J'ai croisé l'autre jour votre amie Madame Bliss chez Madame Hennessy mais trop rapidement pour pouvoir lui parler de vous. Pas assez cependant pour qu'elle ne m'ait demandé un renseignement littéraire." Thus, by exception to ordinary rules, both husband and wife were keen and perceptive collectors, with tastes concentrated on objects and styles not widely recognized at the time.

Royall Tyler (1884–1953), for many years their close friend and ally in collecting, was a scholar of remarkable perceptions and versatility. The son of a Headmaster of Adams Academy, Quincy, Massachusetts, and a descendant of the Royall Tyler who had been both the first

American playwright and an early Chief Justice of Vermont, he had been taken to Europe after his father's death in 1897 and so had been educated at Harrow, New College, Oxford, and the University of Salamanca, rather than at Harvard. Slightly younger than Mildred Barnes, he had known her in New England when they were both practically children. As they shared somewhat precocious intellectual interests, he saw her whenever he returned to the United States during his student years. Understanding what he was trying to do, with the intuition that makes some young women wise beyond their actual years, she counseled him in the somewhat unorthodox pursuit of his studies. From his residence at Salamanca, where Miguel de Unamuno was the great attraction, Royall Tyler came to understand Spain as few foreigners have. Thus in 1909, aged twenty-five, he published a first book, *Spain, a Study of Her Life and Arts*, that after more than fifty years is still a perceptive and useful introduction to the country. He then became Editor of the Calendar of State Papers relating to the negotiations between England and Spain that was being published by the British Government as a guide to documents in the Public Record Office. In the end he prepared five massive volumes, dealing with the reigns of Edward VI and Queen Mary, the first of which appeared in 1913. His fondness for Spain led him to the study of Byzantine art, a field then little understood or appreciated. Few scholars have combined with their learning such imagination, aesthetic intuition, and personal charm in the ordinary affairs of life. When the Blisses were ordered to Paris in 1912, Royall Tyler was settled there with his Italian wife and infant son. Thus constant meetings, strolls along quais, and visits to *antiquaires* with him enlivened the routine of diplomatic business, beside leading Robert Bliss to his first pre-Columbian purchase and focusing Mildred Bliss's early taste for the Middle Ages — shown in her girlhood enthusiasm for *opus Anglicanum* — upon the art of Byzantium.

The war years in Paris were crowded and strenuous, for while her husband's obligations at the Embassy increased by the week, Mrs. Bliss was busily occupied with the Comité des Enfants de la Frontière that arranged for the housing and education of French boys and girls of the war zone, whose fathers were fighting and whose mothers, if alive, were often sheltered only by the ruins of homes destroyed by the enemy.

After the United States entered the war in 1917 the Comité worked in cooperation not only with the French authorities but with the American Red Cross. Even with these arduous activities, the Blisses had accumulated by the end of their long stay in Paris considerable quantities of books, household effects, and works of art that were hardly adapted to the itinerant nature of life in the Foreign Service.

Towards the end of 1919 they returned to the United States on leave of absence, and in April 1920 Robert Bliss was assigned to the Department of State as Chief of the Division of Western European Affairs. This was the moment when they began to visualize a permanent home for their possessions, to which they might at the appropriate time retire. The big, rambling Blount place in R Street in Georgetown attracted them by its superb location and fine trees and the charming variety of its topographical contours. The house itself left much to be desired, for the Federalist simplicity of its original design had been obscured by the additions and alterations of Linthicums and Blounts. But the lines were good and the shape of the rooms congenial. By removing mid-nineteenth-century mantels, porches, mansard roofs, and other excrescences, the Blisses could restore a suitable shell within which attractive rooms could be created. Above all the variety of levels in the grounds, which fell away steeply towards Rock Creek, suggested infinite possibilities for gardens. Accordingly they bought the place and undertook its thorough renovation.

Soon after, Robert and Mildred Bliss brought their friends Royall Tyler and Beatrix Jones Farrand, the distinguished landscape gardener, to see what they had acquired. Royall Tyler, as always, was talking of Byzantine art, while Mrs. Farrand was thinking aloud of garden potentialities. Thus from the very beginning, the character of Dumbarton Oaks was taking shape. There was everything to be done, but fortunately the Blisses had three years of duty in Washington in which to plan and oversee the initial work, for on 15 March 1921 Mr. Bliss was appointed by President Harding Third Assistant Secretary of State, and in September of that year was designated a member of the United States delegation to the Washington Conference on the Limitation of Armaments. The transformation of Dumbarton Oaks had been well begun by January 1923 when they were once again on the move with his appointment as Minister to Sweden.

As built by William Hammond Dorsey, the house had consisted on the ground floor of two rooms on either side of a large central hall. Edward M. Linthicum had added side wings, the eastward one extending back beyond the north facade of the house. In the new dispensation, the room to the left of the central hall became the dining room, with pantries and kitchen in the west wing. The large room to the right was subdivided into coat and dressing rooms on either side of a passage that led to an exquisitely proportioned oval room with recessed bookcases and eighteenth-century French furniture. The east wing on the front became a less formal library for Mr. Bliss; the space in the ell to the rear was converted into a drawing room. In a long gallery at the back of the house a pair of graceful staircases were introduced, with ironwork of Mrs. Bliss's suggestion that, while recalling eighteenth-century France, actually incorporated certain of the flora and fauna of the place. This major reconstruction, which achieved the form of the present Dumbarton Oaks, was begun in August 1921 from the architectural designs of Frederick H. Brooke. In 1929 a large music room was added in the rear on the west, with an entrance from the stair hall that balanced the mass of the drawing room ell.

The Dumbarton Oaks house, as one sees it today, is essentially the creation of Mr. and Mrs. Bliss in the nineteen twenties and thirties, always in reference to the fine Federalist shell of the 1800 building. Similarly the gardens represent the skill of Mrs. Farrand and Mrs. Bliss in constructing an enchanting landscape out of magnificent existing trees that grew on slopes so varied and in places so steep as to present a great challenge in design. When Mrs. Farrand began studying the site soon after the Blisses had bought the property, she had behind her a good forty years of experience in garden design and creation. At the age of eleven, in 1883, Beatrix Cadwallader Jones had had a hand in laying out the grounds of "Reef Point," her parents' place at Bar Harbor, Maine, which she came to look upon as home for the next seventy-five years. While still in her teens she studied, with professional seriousness, with Professor Charles Sprague Sargent, the founder and first Director of the Arnold Arboretum of Harvard University, through whose efforts many plants were brought from China and other distant countries to New England, where, if sufficiently hardy, they were propagated and introduced into general cultivation. Of this period in Beatrix Jones's life, Mrs. Bliss wrote in *Beatrix Jones Farrand, 1872–1959: An Appreciation of a Great Landscape Gardener*:

Never was a great teacher granted a pupil more ideally suited to his hopes. His knowledge was absorbed by her eager young intelligence, and the elderly Professor Sargent saw his dream of the continuity of horticultural research in this country assured. And then one day the pupil submitted the plan of a garden — paths, benches, group plantings in height and color — and the Professor frowned. "Don't waste time on what you call design. You must hybridize and propagate. The only paths necessary are merely for accessibility and there is no time to sit on benches; a tree stump will do as well."

Later the pupil made one more effort to stir the comprehension of *gardens* as an aim in itself, but the master of horticulture could not understand. Sadly he saw his dream vanish and his beloved pupil leave Jamaica Plain and enter, one might say, her very personal garden gate.

But this very personal garden gate led, not to tasteful ladylike dabbling, but to a highly professional career as a garden designer, with a large office in New York and heavy demand for her work. While still in her twenties she became a charter member and Fellow of the American Society of Landscape Architects. Although in later years she was elected to honorary membership in the American Institute of Architects, she always regarded *architects* as designers of buildings and herself as a *landscape gardener*, for to her landscape was soil, water, and plants, and gardening the arrangement of landscape to delight the eye and the mind. When well past eighty, she recalled how she had "tried to heed Professor Sargent's advice to make the plan fit the ground and not twist the ground to fit a plan, and furthermore to study the tastes of the owner," as well as his admonition to "look at great landscape paintings, to observe and analyze natural beauty, to travel widely . . . and learn from all the great arts, as all art is akin."

In 1913 Beatrix Jones married the Yale historian Max Farrand, who a few years later became director of the Henry E. Huntington Library and Art Gallery at San Marino, California. Even after her base shifted from her native New York to California, Beatrix Farrand continued the practice of her profession not only for private owners but as consulting landscape gardener for Princeton, Yale, Oberlin, the University of Chicago, and other academic institutions.

In her tribute to Beatrix Farrand, Mrs. Bliss wrote:

The gardens of Dumbarton Oaks were perhaps one of the most difficult problems presented to her, for she found not only an existing and rather dominating house and an unusually wide variety of grades, but also the very definite personal preferences of the owners with their special interest in design and texture. The gardens were to be for spring and autumn enjoyment and in winter to have perennial green in abundance. A swimming pool, tennis court, and brook completed the illusion of country life, while clever planting bordering the lawn screened the street on the south side and left the birds undisturbed.

The situation was described in greater detail by the British landscape architect, Lanning Roper, writing for the *Journal of the Royal Horticultural Society* in July 1959.

The house, built in 1801 and Georgian in conception, commands a fine position on a high rise of ground. It faces south with tree-shaded lawns stretching gently down to the road which fronts it and in a long sweep to the south-east. On the east end of the house is a long, low Orangery housing a collection of ferns and tropical plants. To the east and north the land slopes sharply. At the bottom of the valley is a charming stream, the water falling gently over the small rocky outcrops. This stream today forms part of the park as does the wooded hillside on the far side with its magnificent stand of native trees including oaks, maples, beeches, sycamores and tulip trees. It is this lovely woodland of the park and of adjoining estates that provides the superb outlook from the series of terraces and overlooks which are as important to the beauty of the garden as are the noble trees, giant specimen boxwoods and flowers within it. Moreover, the sky above forms a vast backdrop and this, too, was very much in the minds of Mrs. Bliss and of Beatrix Farrand, her landscape architect, who is considered by many to be the Gertrude Jekyll of America.

I say minds, as the gardens of Dumbarton Oaks are so much a product of the happy co-operation and harmony of ideas of these two dynamic minds. Through their very close co-operation the garden evolved, each conceiving, adapting and re-evaluating her own ideas in the light of experience and the best considered opinion of the other. Mrs. Bliss knew from the start what she wanted to create, for she had definite conceptions, some of which she had treasured from childhood; others were inspired by her varied travels, for she loved to take ideas, designs and even actual details of ornament and architecture for adaptation to the peculiar needs of Dumbarton Oaks. Mrs. Farrand had taste, the "know how" and the courage of her convictions as well as unflagging energy — all important characters for such a partnership.

When Mr. and Mrs. Bliss purchased the house in 1920 with its fine oaks, maples and tulip trees (*Liriodendron tulipifera*) certain basic principles were laid down for Mrs. Farrand. First the gardens were to be essentially formal with strong accent on design. As Dumbarton Oaks was to be a permanent town residence there must be year-round interest with a predominance of evergreens, both coniferous and broad-leaved. These with deciduous trees and shrubs were to form the frame for the flowers which were to be carefully chosen for colour and form to enhance the scheme but which were never to dominate it. Furthermore certain sections of the garden were to be entirely green with ground covers chosen for contrasting leaf forms, colours and textures, as this charming conception of trees planted to form a high arched alley, feathery backgrounds, reflecting pools, and winding paths started in childhood as an ideal dream and as the years passed it was to become an *idée fixe*. Its eventual realization is epitomized in Lover's Lane Pool with its little stepped amphitheatre, and Melisande's Alley. Because of the dramatic slope of the site it was obvious that the garden must consist of a series of broad terraces leading from the strictly formal architectural character of the house through various transitions to the delightful informality of the lower garden with its loose plantings of flowering trees, shrubs and naturalized bulbs. Full advantage was to be taken of the fine view and the sweep of sky. Lastly Mrs. Bliss wished to incorporate into the garden a wealth of ornament executed in a variety of media to illustrate the wide range of decorative architectural detail and ornament available to the gardener.

As planning for the gardens had to proceed from the house outwards, the first step was the designing of the east terraces that would lead down the hillside. Since Mr. Bliss was appointed Minister to Sweden in January, 1923, the tremendous work of cutting out the terraces, moving earth, and building retaining walls and drainage systems, had to be carried out during the owners' long absence in Stockholm. As he was made Ambassador to Argentina in 1927, Mr. and Mrs. Bliss were away from Washington during the first ten years of the creation of the Dumbarton Oaks gardens. But they kept in close touch with the progress of work, and whenever they returned to this country on leave, however briefly, new decisions were taken. Details of materials, patterns for the construction of walls and pavements, temporary mock-ups of garden ornaments and wrought-iron gates and grilles were endlessly set up, taken down, and altered, as Mrs. Farrand and Mrs. Bliss continued, through the process of trial and error, to seek the ideal solution in scale and material for each and every problem, however minute. It is never easy for such perfectionists as both women were to achieve an ideal when joint decisions must be made by people separated by an ocean. Yet the evolution of the Dumbarton Oaks gardens was harmonious and happy, for, as Mrs. Bliss has written.

Such were Mrs. Farrand's integrity and loyalty that, despite the long absences necessitated by the professional nomadism of the owners, never in all the years did she impose a detail of which she was "sure" but which the owners did not "see"; and never were the owners so persuasive as to insist on a design which Mrs. Farrand's inner eye could not accept. A deepening friendship born of intellectual challenges, of differing tastes and of the generous tact of her rich wisdom made the years of their close association a singularly happy and most nourishing experience. Never did Beatrix Farrand impose on the land an arbitrary concept. She "listened" to the light and wind and grade of each area under study. The gardens grew naturally from one another until now, in their luxuriant spring growth, as in the winter when leafless branches show each degree of distance and the naked masonry (from brick and limestone near the house, through brick and gray stone in the rose garden, towards stone only in the fountain terrace, and finally to the stone and wood leading to the apple orchard), there is a special quality of charming restfulness recognized by thousands of yearly visitors.

The four years that the Blisses spent in Stockholm were pleasant from every point of view, for the pair made lasting friendships among the scholars, scientists, and artists who abound in Sweden. Moreover it was not difficult to continue the ties that they had earlier formed in Paris. Mr. Bliss's designation as Ambassador to Argentina in 1927 took him and his wife into a scene very different from Stockholm. Although it was by no means unfamiliar, since they had lived in Buenos Aires for two years and a half before going to Paris, in 1927 the post offered considerable challenge even to diplomatic friendliness. As he wrote subsequently in a Harvard class report:

Here every sort of obstruction lay across the path of the new American Ambassador, including bombings by Sacco-Vanzetti adherents, a hypercritical Press and constant allusions to the United States troops still in Nicaragua. What the State Department tried to construct one day our Department of Agriculture tore down the next, culminating in the disastrous Hawley-Smoot tariff. Fiery misinterpretations of the Monroe Doctrine in various legislative bodies fed the antagonisms. Meantime Argentina was undergoing an internal strain which accentuated animosities. I had the unusual experience of dealing with a Minister of Foreign Affairs who was not permitted by his President to set foot in the American Embassy. This would eventually have become intolerable had one not scented the gathering storm which broke late in 1930, deposing the leftist President Irigoyen and placing conservative General Uriburu at the helm. The door barely ajar previously was now fully opened, relations improved and when I left Buenos Aires three years later the Press was almost entirely friendly.

Even at this distance, and with these preoccupations, work progressed on the Dumbarton Oaks gardens and music room, and some important Byzantine objects were acquired for the collection that was eventually to be housed there. Although in 1924, at the request of the League of Nations, Royall Tyler went to Budapest to spend some years as financial adviser to the Hungarian government, he actively continued his studies of Byzantine art. In collaboration with his state-of-Maine friend, Hayford Peirce, brother of the painter Waldo Peirce, he wrote *Byzantine Art*, published in London in 1926, and a larger two volume work, *L'Art byzantin*, that appeared in Paris in 1932. Moreover, in addition to untangling the finances of Hungary, he took an active part in the planning of the great Byzantine exposition held at the Louvre in the summer of 1931, in which more examples of the arts in all media were assembled, from public and private collections, than had been together in one place since the fall of Constantinople half a millennium before. Royall Tyler's lively letters, whether from Budapest or Paris, brought Europe nearer to Buenos Aires and provided Robert and Mildred Bliss with news that made it possible for them to continue collecting, even at long range.

In 1924, while still in Sweden, they had bought the great sixth-century silver paten, recently found at Riha in Syria, on which the Communion of the Apostles is represented in repoussé. Behind an altar covered with a loosely draped heavy cloth stand two figures of Christ, offering simultaneously bread and wine to the Apostles, who are divided into two groups that approach with reverent inclination. The figures, the altar cloth and vessels, and part of the architectural background are gilded, and on the raised rim is a Greek inscription in niello, reading: "For the repose [of the souls] of Sergia, the daughter of Ioannes, and Theodosios and the salvation of Megalos and Nonnos and their children." While the subject is Christian, the feeling is still Hellenistic. From the same Riha treasure, Royall Tyler secured for his own collection a silver chalice, similar in form to one represented on the altar on the paten.

In 1929, while in Buenos Aires, Mr. and Mrs. Bliss obtained another of the most dramatic objects in the Dumbarton Oaks collection — the large sixth-century Coptic wool tapestry of Hestia Polyolbos, the goddess or personification of the hearth, who is hieratically enthroned between two attendants and six putti holding medallions inscribed in Greek with the names of the rich blessings she distributes: wealth, joy, praise, abundance, virtue, and progress. This singularly beautiful tapestry, woven in shades of rose, blue, green, and buff, offers a pagan counterpart to the contemporaneous Christian scene of the Riha paten. But while the Communion of the Apostles has much of the life, motion, and sculptural quality of the classical tradition, the pagan Hestia is enthroned in the static manner of a Byzantine mosaic. Other textiles acquired during these years included the Coptic wool and linen panel on which two Nereids ride sea monsters with lively enthusiasm, and the eighth-century Byzantine silk fragment of the "elephant tamer," in which a figure holds the trunks of two elephants in frozen heraldic symmetry.

In 1928 the Blisses bought a third-century gold necklace formed of forty links of paired ducks with a clasp of paired dolphins surmounted by a shell and an early seventh-century Egyptian necklace of biconical beads, alternately in gold and lapis lazuli, with a pendant in the form of a lapis lazuli shell framing a gold figurine of Aphrodite in high relief, as well as gold and jewelled Roman necklaces and pins of the fifth century from a treasure excavated in 1910 near the Piazza della Consolazione in Rome.

The Riha paten, the textiles, and some of the jewelry were lent to the 1931 Byzantine exposition at the Louvre, where they took high rank among the privately owned objects. To balance such an elegant pagan frippery as the Aphrodite necklace, the Blisses acquired in 1933 the Carolingian chalice of Grimfridus, that was in its way as rare as the Riha paten. This ninth-century liturgical vessel was made of copper alloy, gilded, with silver inlay decorations on the cup, which are repeated in reverse on the foot. Formerly known as the chalice of Saint Chrodegand, through a dubious eighteenth-century association of the vessel with that eighth-century bishop of Séz in Normandy, it was once in the treasure of the priory of Saint-Martin des Champs. Later it was successively in the Basilewsky collection in Paris and in the Hermitage Museum in Petrograd.

All these objects were as provocative as they were rare and unfamiliar. It would be difficult to find a comparable number that display more clearly the religious and artistic crosscurrents, the similarities and contradictions of the art of the first millennium of the Christian era, or that would better repay careful study.

CHAPTER VII

Dumbarton Oaks Occupied

BY 1931 Robert Bliss had decided to retire two years later at the expiration of thirty-three years of diplomatic service, and so informed President Hoover. Before the election of November 1932 he wrote the President, reminding him of this request, and soon afterwards received the answer: "You will have to resign to someone else." This he did, leaving Argentina in 1933, and, incidentally, becoming the first Foreign Service Officer to retire with the rank of Ambassador and to receive a pension. Thus after more than a dozen years of ownership, he and his wife were for the first time able to settle permanently in the country house that they had created in the city of Washington.

A decade of garden construction and planting had indeed produced an extraordinary illusion of country surroundings. From the windows of the dining room and library on the south (entrance) side of the house, one looked across a broad sweep of lawns, divided by the curving driveway leading in from R Street. The road was completely screened by a wall and by shrubbery planted within it that thickened the cover under the taller deciduous trees. The north facade of the main body of the house, whose windows on two floors lighted the galleries containing the double stairways, looked onto the North Court, partly enclosed by the flanking wings of the drawing room and music room, which gave on the North Vista. There three rectangular lawns on different levels, gradually narrowing in width, led to a point of view above a steep drop, from which one saw only sky and the trees of the distant hillside on the other side of the valley. Areas even on approximately similar levels were subdivided by walls to create intimate "rooms," like the Star Garden, north of the drawing room, with its Aquarius fountain and Zodiac circle and the inscription from Chaucer's translation of Boethius: "O Thou

Maker of the Whele that Bereth the Starres, and tornest the Hevens with a ravishing sweigh."

From the Star Garden one passed to the terrace of the Green Garden, north of the Orangery, from which a choice of directions was offered. Many feet below, to the north, a swimming pool surrounded by a paved terrace, had been created on the side of an old manure pit. A vaulted loggia, with wisterias growing over its facade, and dressing rooms, built under the upper terrace, had replaced the cow-sheds of earlier owners. A flight of steps leading down to the level of the pool divided around a baroque fountain, consisting of a shell on a travertine pedestal. At the west end of the pool terrace, a wall fountain set in a niche was shaded by weeping cherries, behind which rose a much taller central cedar. Along the north of this terrace stood a line of great pollarded willows, whose weeping branches were reflected in the blue water. These willows are one of the delights of the garden in late winter, when the color of fresh shoots is just beginning to show. In spring one looks through their branches to the flowering crabs and fruit trees on the lower slope. Adjacent to the pool, on a slightly lower level, was a well screened tennis court.

To the east of the Green Garden, a series of formal terraces took one down the hillside by gradual stages. Each has its distinct character. The Beech Terrace, created around a great purple beech, was made intimate and useful by the presence of pink marble benches and a table; the Urn Terrace, next below, as originally planned, had a great stone urn standing in the center of box-edged parterres. A broad flight of steps led to the much larger Rose Terrace, twelve feet below, with great specimen box bushes and rose beds. A gate in the south walls opened on a path that led to the East Lawn, or, past the Terrier Column, on to the Lover's Lane Pool in the woods. But the obvious direction to follow was down a double staircase to the Fountain Terrace, to the north of which was originally an herb garden, later transformed into a paved Pot Garden, with a wisteria-covered arbor, built after a design of du Cerceau. Thus far progress had been by formal flights of steps between terraces. From here paths curved down the hillside in various directions.

To the north, on a lower hillside, lay the herbaceous borders, framed in yews cut with peaked tops to avoid damage from snow, beyond which were the cutting and kitchen gardens. To the eastward another path curved to the enchanting woodland area near Lover's Lane, the eastern boundary of the property. There in a natural glade, some 55 feet below the Beech Terrace, was Lover's Lane Pool, approached by a winding brick path at the upper end, where a minuscule baroque amphitheatre — of bricks laid under Mrs. Farrand's personal supervision — looked down across the pool to Melisande's Alley, where a double line of silver maples, arching high overhead, led still further down the hill, following the line of an old cow path.

Other slopes of the hillside were massed with forsythia, flowering cherries, and other delights of spring, while in the bottom of the valley were natural woodland paths, where early spring bulbs created a carpet reminiscent of a Fra Angelico celestial meadow. Areas were linked together with great cunning to provide an infinite variety of changing moods. From the Urn Terrace one could, for example, proceed sharply down hill by the brick-paved Box Walk, leaving the tennis court to port and the herbaceous and kitchen gardens to starboard, to reach the Ellipse, where a broad fountain was set in a vast ellipse of box. Open space or woods, colored bloom or varieties of green, formality or the opposite, could almost instantly be achieved by varying one's course. While given spots enjoyed their supreme moments according to season, all had some attraction at any time in the year. Moreover the gardens lent themselves equally happily to generous hospitality or solitary reflection. Six hundred guests could mill about as pleasantly at the State Department garden party each June as Secretary Cordell Hull could quietly play his afternoon game of croquet on the North Vista. And always there was the pleasant illusion of being in the country.

The house had the same versatile flexibility as the gardens. While the owners and a few friends could stay there with the sensation of a comfortable intimacy, there was ample possibility for entertainment on a generous scale. This was achieved by a variety of sizes and moods in the first floor rooms. The exquisitely proportioned little oval salon on the front of the house, with its Ionic pilasters, recessed shelves of French books, and Savonnerie rug, was designed for intimate formality. The large drawing room in the northeast wing had in its west wall two windows overlooking the North Court; an alcove opposite, containing

Mrs. Bliss's writing desk, had multiple windows that brought the room into close relation with the Green Garden terrace. Originally the drawing room contained four large Hubert Robert landscapes, set in the panelling, but as books soon overflowed from the oak-panelled library on the front of the house, these paintings were moved to the adjacent stair gallery, and their places taken by tall recessed bookcases.

The music room, added in 1929, was in a northwest wing on the opposite side of the North Court from the drawing room. From the stair gallery one entered it by going down eight wide steps through a passage decorated with mural paintings by Allyn Cox. A sixteenth-century stone chimney piece from the Château of Théobon, Loubés-Bernac, near Duras (Lot-et-Garonne) and two sixteenth-century Italian red Verona marble arches established the proportion of the room, which had a wooden ceiling painted in the manner of the French sixteenth century, similar to one at the Château de Chimerey. The height of the room was sufficient to accommodate a 1460 Tournai tapestry showing the Prince of Malice seated on his throne surrounded by personifications of the Vices, while to the left the Virtues proceed from the gates of their castle, convoyed by three angels. There were also a small sixteenth-century Flemish tapestry of Christ and the Virgin, very finely woven with liberal use of gold and silver thread, and a large Renaissance tapestry representing the month of April, woven at Brussels about 1525–30 from a cartoon of Bernard van Orley. Most of the furniture was Italian and Spanish of the sixteenth and seventeenth centuries, the most monumental piece being a walnut cabinet from a villa at Caprarola, near Rome, with eight doors decorated in itarsia work of floral design, and the inscription "QUIESCIT ANIMA LIBRIS" on the cornice. Among the paintings was a Florentine Madonna and Child by Bernardo Daddi of about 1335, the portrait of a princess of the house of Savoy by the fifteenth-century Maitre de Flémalle, and an El Greco Visitation. Sculpture included French and German Gothic Madonnas, a Chinese bronze owl of the Chou period, a T'ang stone head, a Sung seated Lohan carved in wood, a bronze Egyptian cat of the late Dynastic period, and an engaging Egyptian wooden figurine of a dancing girl of the Twelfth Dynasty.

The grand piano in the music room was a fine Steinway that had

belonged to Mrs. Bliss's mother and had been brought to Dumbarton
Oaks after her death. Paderewski, who had played it in Santa Barbara
in 1927, had signed his name on the instrument. In this room Wanda
Landowska and Ralph Kirkpatrick were often at the harpsichord, and
Stravinsky conducted his Dumbarton Oaks Concerto, commissioned in
1937 by Mr. and Mrs. Bliss; while Nadia Boulanger, who was often
to be seen in the depths of the gardens — a splendid walker with head
erect and flat heeled shoes — would later come here to lead her group
of singers or instrumentalists with one hand while playing the piano
accompaniment with the other. Lucrezia Bori sang here, accompanied
by Ernst Schelling, whose frequent presence was a very enriching
element in the scene. A bronze head of Schelling done by Malvina
Hoffman in 1940, which is now in the Garden Library, is a permanent
reminder of his friendship with Mr. and Mrs. Bliss. There was a
constant flow of music at Dumbarton Oaks. Soli, duos, trios, quartets,
quintets, sextets, septets, and octets exemplified the evolution of chamber music.

The music room also provided a congenial setting for conversation
on a great variety of themes. One Christmas Alexis Carrel sat by the
fire there as he talked of the evolution of surgery, while on other
occasions Henry Fairfield Osborn came to tell of biological mysteries.
Blériot, the aviator who first flew the English Channel, some years later
gave an illustrated lecture on his exploit in the music room, showing
the Edwardian crowd awaiting his landing, and, with a long pointer,
directing the attention of his audience to the pilot, whom he called,
anonymously if not humbly, "Le Héro."

Robert and Mildred Bliss drew to Dumbarton Oaks old friends of all
ages and many professions. And in the course of achieving details in the
creation of the place, they developed happy relationships with artists
they had not previously known. In January 1965, in writing to my old
friend the engraver Rudolph Ruzicka, who had designed their book-
plates, I casually mentioned that Mrs. Bliss had recently asked me to
undertake this sketch of Dumbarton Oaks. Soon after, he replied:

It will be thirty years next July when I received a telegram from Mrs. Bliss
asking me to come to Washington to do some drawings of Dumbarton Oaks

Gardens. Since I never heard of either the Gardens or Mrs. Bliss I went with some reluctance. I spent a week at Dumbarton Oaks, overwhelmed by the unaccustomed splendor of my quarters and by the warm friendliness of the Blisses.

I always retained the warmest regard for Mrs. Bliss. When I saw her in Washington six years ago she still remembered me and appeared, miraculously, unchanged.

Scholars, as well as artists and musicians, found their way to Dumbarton Oaks. The Byzantinist Thomas Whittemore might be there, fresh from a scaffolding several hundred feet above the floor of Hagia Sophia, where he had been carrying on the work he had initiated — or, one might almost say, invented — of freeing the Christian mosaics and frescoes from the plaster and cement with which the Turks had covered them more than four hundred years before. So might Henri Focillon of the Collège de France, noble medieval scholar and familiar friend of all literatures and all arts, or Edward W. Forbes, Paul J. Sachs, or Wilhelm R. W. Koehler from Harvard, or Charles Rufus Morey from Princeton, or Michael Ivanovich Rostovtzeff, or Doro Levi, for the growing Byzantine collection, combined with the conversation and surroundings, was a powerful attraction.

The objects from Dumbarton Oaks lent to "The Dark Ages" exhibition and seminar, organized by Francis Henry Taylor at the Worcester Art Museum in late February 1937, illustrate the growth of the collection. There the Riha paten was accompanied by a sixth-century Syrian silver flabellum, or liturgical fan, that Mr. and Mrs. Bliss had acquired in 1936. This was decorated with the winged creatures and flaming wheels of the vision of Ezekiel. With the tapestries of Nereids and of Hestia, which had been shown in the Paris exhibition of 1931, was lent an Alexandrian silk fabric of the sixth century (acquired in 1934), decorated with four repetitive rows of confronted figures of Samson wrenching the jaws of a rearing lion. Ivory carving was represented by three very different objects (added in 1935, 1936, and 1937): the consular diptych of Flavius Theodoros Filoxenus of the year 525, formerly in the Trivulzio collection in Milan; the sixth-century Egyptian circular pyxis, decorated with representations of Moses receiving the Law and of Daniel in the lions' den, from the treasure of the abbey of Moggio in the Veneto;

and the Byzantine late-tenth-century plaque of the Dormition of the Virgin. The art of barbarians in their wild state was represented by Visigothic bronze fibulae in the form of birds, sheathed in gold leaf with garnet insets, and in their Christianized domestication, by the chalice of Grimfridus.

The pace of collecting, which was considerably accelerated in 1936 and 1937, reached its peak in the years 1938 and 1940. By the latter year the collection included not only a representative group of Byzantine objects in many materials, but pieces that illustrated the derivation of the style from classical antiquity and exemplified the extraneous elements brought into the Empire by barbarian invaders. For example, among the seven pieces of sculpture in bronze or stone acquired in 1936 were a Greek bronze statuette of Hephaistos of the fifth century, B.C., the huge Roman sarcophagus of the fourth century, A.D., representing the Seasons, formerly in the Barberini collection in Rome, a marble sixth-century Byzantine relief of a deer grazing, and south Italian marble reliefs of the eleventh or twelfth century depicting stylized birds. The following year a twelfth-century relief of a Byzantine Emperor in a roundel was added; in 1938 came two of the great glories of the collection — the spirited rearing bronze horse of the sixth century, found at Senaa, the capital of Yemen, South Arabia, and the large eleventh-century marble relief of the Virgin, standing in an attitude of intercession. Related to the latter in mood, although radically different in scale and material, was the ivory group, acquired in 1939, of the Virgin of the Hodegetria type, holding the Christ child on her left arm, standing between St. John the Baptist and a holy bishop.

From the excavations at Antioch, undertaken in 1932 by a joint expedition of Princeton University, the Louvre, the Worcester and Baltimore Museums, and the Syrian government, came monumental mosaics representing Erotes fishing and riding dolphins, hunting scenes, and the like; capitals, stele, and fragments of inscriptions. But many of the smaller objects, like the mysterious cast-gold figurine of a man — probably made in Gaul in the late fourth or early fifth century, and found about 1928 near a bridge at Le Mans — came to Dumbarton Oaks through the persistent searches made by Mr. and Mrs. Bliss and Royall Tyler among the *antiquaires* of western Europe. Thus objects of all kinds of metals, bone, wood, glass, ceramics, porphyry, agate, and crystal came to join the sculpture, the ivories, and the textiles.

To make sense out of the collections, a considerable working library was assembled. Thus by the late thirties, in addition to the widely varied works of art that adorned the house and the equally varied books that had been accumulated for the sheer pleasure of reading, Dumbarton Oaks contained the makings of a unique research collection in the Byzantine field. The collection was, moreover, considerably used by the small group of scholars, American and European, whose imaginations led them into these comparatively uncharted waters. Just as Mrs. John Lowell Gardner had created Fenway Court in Boston in the early years of the century with the clear intention that it should upon her death become the Isabella Stewart Gardner Museum, so Mr. and Mrs. Bliss built up the library and collection and developed the gardens of Dumbarton Oaks with a definite plan for their perpetuation. There was, however, an important difference. Fenway Court was to be a museum, pure and simple, maintained (through an independent board of trustees) as its owner had created it, down to the last detail. Dumbarton Oaks, on the contrary, was envisioned as a research center integrated with the scholarly activities of Harvard University, and susceptible to indefinite growth. The initial steps towards this end had already been taken with President A. Lawrence Lowell before his retirement in 1933. The decision to accelerate the transfer was succinctly described by Mr. Bliss in the 45th anniversary report of his Harvard class of 1900.

As the depression increased and Nazism gained control of Germany we knew war was a certainty and that inevitably this country would be sucked into the cataclysm. So we faced the future squarely and decided to transfer Dumbarton Oaks to the University in 1940. To ease the wrench, we assured each other that freedom of choice is a privilege not often granted by Fate and that to give up our home at our own time to assure the long range realization of our plan was the way of wisdom. Thus we are enjoying the transformation of Dumbarton Oaks into an institution — the only one of its particular sort in existence.

In preparation for the transfer, a wing was added, extending from the music room to the 32nd Street boundary of the property. This consisted of two pavilions opening on an enclosed courtyard, connected at either end by glazed loggias. The court was on axis with the western window of the music room. The southern pavilion provided a public entrance from 32nd Street, without reference to the main house, as well as offices and a corridor, lighted from the courtyard, for the display of textiles. From this entrance, a glazed loggia, in which some of the Antioch mosaics were installed, led along the western end of the court-yard to the north pavilion, which was designed as a gallery for the Byzantine Collection. On the west wall various pieces of sculpture were displayed on brackets. The east wall was dominated by the Barberini Seasons sarcophagus, with the tapestry of Hestia Polyolbos above it. Glazed floor and wall cases contained the smaller objects. From this gallery, and from the textile corridor in the south pavilion, quarter-circular passages led agreeably into the music room. This architectural solution for converting a private house into the beginning of a learned institution was as ingenious in its way as some of the transformations from hillside to terraces that had occurred in the gardens. A scholar working in the main house had only pleasantly to traverse the music room to reach the Byzantine gallery. Conversely visitors to the gallery, or persons coming to concerts or lectures, could enter from 32nd Street without penetrating the working areas of the house at all. The music room was left unchanged, in the confident hope that it would continue to be used as it had been in the past.

By 1940 the research library contained a carefully chosen nucleus of about fourteen thousand volumes that included the most important works on Byzantine art and archaeology, museum catalogues, illus-trative material on manuscripts, painting, mosaics, sculpture, and the minor arts, and runs of the principal learned journals and periodicals in art and archaeology. This collection was concentrated in the new south pavilion. In the library on the first floor of the main house, some five thousand volumes on Western European art, mostly assembled before the development of the specialized research collection, were left as they had been, as were various French books that lined the walls of the Oval Room. Some thousands of other rare books, autograph letters, and lit-erary manuscripts that had been scattered in various parts of the house were assembled in the drawing room. Otherwise Mr. and Mrs. Bliss left the house substantially as they had occupied it, for such evolution as might prove necessary.

With these preparations completed, Robert and Mildred Bliss deeded

Dumbarton Oaks on 29 November 1940 to the President and Fellows of Harvard College, complete with collections, library, and furnishings. Although the greater part of the gardens accompanied the gift, some 27 acres, comprising the lower valley with its naturalized planting, were set aside for public enjoyment as the Dumbarton Oaks Park. This area, entered by following Lover's Lane from R Street, is now under the care of the National Park Service. Having thus achieved their purpose, Mr. and Mrs. Bliss took themselves to Montecito, California. The final chapter in the private ownership of Dumbarton Oaks having been completed, the nature of its new career can best be indicated by quoting the dedicatory inscription placed on the exterior wall of the Byzantine gallery on 32nd Street:

QUOD SEVERIS METES

THE

DUMBARTON OAKS

RESEARCH LIBRARY AND COLLECTION

HAS BEEN ASSEMBLED AND CONVEYED TO

HARVARD UNIVERSITY

BY MILDRED AND ROBERT WOODS BLISS

THAT THE CONTINUITY OF SCHOLARSHIP IN THE

BYZANTINE AND MEDIAEVAL HUMANITIES

MAY REMAIN UNBROKEN

TO CLARIFY AN EVER CHANGING PRESENT

AND TO INFORM THE FUTURE

WITH WISDOM

MCMXL

CHAPTER VIII

Quod Severis Metes

THE parable, so succinct in Latin, that was placed at the head of the dedicatory inscription and carved elsewhere in the gardens — "As ye sow, so shall ye reap" — was indeed highly pertinent to Dumbarton Oaks. Sheaves of wheat that symbolize it appear in wrought-iron gates and other decorative elements throughout the place. The seed had been generously and well sown. It germinated quickly, and good husbandmen were not lacking. But the grain ripened more slowly than the sowers and the husbandmen had hoped, because of the heavy storms that broke soon after the first appearance of shoots above the ground.

The first formal act of the Dumbarton Oaks Research Library and Collection took place on 2 and 3 November 1940 when Mr. Bliss made a brief speech presenting the place to Harvard, Edward W. Forbes and Paul J. Sachs accepted it on behalf of the university, and four inaugural lectures were delivered by eminent scholars who had often frequented the house in earlier years. Henri Focillon spoke on "Préhistoire et Moyen Age," Michael Ivanovich Rostovtzeff on "The Near East in the Hellenistic and Roman Times," Charles Rufus Morey on "The Early Christian Ivories of the Eastern Empire," and Wilhelm R. W. Koehler on "Byzantine Art in the West." No precise pattern existed for the development of such an institution, but it is always sound practice to bring mature scholars and younger men of promise together in quiet surroundings with plenty of books and let nature take its course. The appointment of Morey and Focillon as the first Senior Research Fellows was a logical step in this direction. Of all American medievalists, Charles Rufus Morey, through his studies of the Museo Cristiano in the Vatican, possessed the greatest familiarity with Byzantine objects of the type represented in the Dumbarton Oaks Collection. Moreover, at Princeton he had been both the inspirer of younger scholars and the developer of the Index of Christian Art, which attempted to unravel the tangled iconography of the Early Christian and Medieval periods. Henri Focillon, a *Normalien* long Professor at the Collège de France, combined with perceptive knowledge of the Middle Ages broad sympathies with all the arts and humanities. This blending of talents represented an auspicious beginning for the new institution.

When Mr. and Mrs. Bliss gave Dumbarton Oaks to Harvard University, they promptly moved to California, leaving the house completely furnished and staffed for its new institutional occupants. Professor and Madame Focillon installed themselves in quarters on the second floor, as did Dr. John Seymour Thacher, the present Director, who had come from the Fogg Museum in November 1940 to act as Executive Director on behalf of Harvard University. Although living in Princeton, Professor Morey, often accompanied by his wife, made frequent trips to Dumbarton Oaks, during which they too occupied quarters on the second floor. But after a few months it became apparent that major structural changes were required for the orderly and efficient operation of the newly established Center for Byzantine Studies. Thus during the summer of 1941 the master bedrooms, baths, and sitting rooms on the front of the second floor of the main house were converted into a large reading room with adjacent offices, and the working books were moved there. At the same time a residence for Dr. Thacher was provided in a separate house in the grounds. Thus within the first year Dumbarton Oaks began to take on the character of an institution, although all changes were made with suitable regard for the design of the house and gardens.

Although Professor Morey's duties at Princeton made it impossible for him to continue as a Senior Research Fellow, it was confidently hoped that Henri Focillon, who could not return to France because of the German occupation, would be able to continue in residence indefinitely. As soon as Focillon came to live at Dumbarton Oaks he immediately turned his remarkable mind to the creation of the learned institution that was envisaged. Unfortunately failing health obliged him to leave before the end of 1941. On 18 November 1941 he gave a last public lecture on the sombre theme: "L'An Mille et la Fin du Monde."

The apocalyptic note of Focillon's last lecture was prophetic, for in less than three weeks Pearl Harbor was attacked, and many plans had to be suspended for the duration. The collections were packed and carried away to places of safety. Until the spring of 1946 the National Defense Research Committee, headed by Dr. Vannevar Bush, which required a secluded place for its vital scientific deliberations, occupied the two pavilions in the 32nd Street wing, as well as the basement and certain of the study rooms on the second floor of the main house. Dr. Thacher, the Executive Officer, was soon called to duty in the United States Naval Reserve but, as he was stationed in Washington, continued to live in his house and was able to keep an eye on Dumbarton Oaks after hours and on Sundays. For the time being, Harvard sent such eminent members of its faculty as the art historian Wilhelm R. W. Koehler, the Byzantine historian Robert P. Blake, the theologian George La Piana, and the urbane classicist, Edward Kennard Rand, who was equally at home in the middle ages, to Dumbarton Oaks for periods of residence as Senior Fellows.

The musical tradition was continued through the war years by occasional concerts by the Musical Art Quartet, the Stradivarius Quartet, and on 10 December 1943 the harpsichordist Wanda Landowska. On that evening she seemed to be translated by emotion, and played as never before. Among the guests were two men, unknown to Mr. and Mrs. Bliss, who, when Wanda Landowska had finished playing, rose from their seats, went over to the piano in the Palladian window of the music room, clicked their heels, bowed low, and returned to their places with tears streaming down their cheeks. They were survivors of the Warsaw massacre.

Although Dumbarton Oaks was already widely known among Byzantine scholars, its name became familiar throughout the world because of the series of informal conferences on the general question of international organization for the maintenance of peace and security that were held there in the summer and early autumn of 1944. The Department of State moved in on 17 July 1944 to make preliminary arrangements for the conversations that were to take place between men of high position in the foreign offices, the diplomatic service, and the armies and navies of allied governments. The first phase of the conversations, which extended from 21 August to 28 September, was between the United States, the United Kingdom, and the Soviet Union; the second phase, from 29 September to 7 October, involved the United States, the United Kingdom, and China. Under Secretary of State Edward R. Stettinius, Jr., headed the United States representatives and Ambassador Andrei A. Gromyko the Soviet Group. The British Group was led during the first phase by Sir Alexander Cadogan and during the second by the Right Honorable the Earl of Halifax, British Ambassador to the United States. The representatives of China were under the chairmanship of Dr. V. K. Wellington Koo, Ambassador to the United Kingdom. The conference was of manageable dimensions, for no national group contained more than twenty persons, including technical advisers and secretaries.

From the Dumbarton Oaks Conference emerged the seed of the United Nations as a permanent organization. On the morning of 21 August, Secretary of State Cordell Hull opened the conversations in the music room with an address in which he declared:

Peace, like liberty, requires constant devotion and ceaseless vigilance. . . . But peace also requires institutions through which the will to peace can be translated into action. The devising of such institutions is a challenge to the wisdom and ingenuity of men and women everywhere. This is why the United Nations, in the midst of a relentless prosecution of the war, have been working together to create the international foundations for a just and lasting peace.

For the next six weeks, the British, Soviet, and American representatives, under the permanent chairmanship of Mr. Stettinius, worked arduously, sometimes in plenary sessions in the music room, but more often in smaller groups, for the conversations at Dumbarton Oaks — informal and exploratory — were, in Sir Alexander Cadogan's graphic phrase, at the "humble official level." For such purposes the various rooms of Dumbarton Oaks, as well as the terraces of the gardens, offered a comfortable and appropriately peaceful setting. The first phase ended with a plenary session on 28 September, at which each of the groups expressed satisfaction with what had been accomplished and with the fine spirit of the discussions. The Soviet Group then went home, and on 29 September the Chinese representatives entered into the second phase of the deliberations. Lord Halifax closed the final plenary session of 7 October with these moving words:

A great Greek philosopher said that the State came into existence in order that men might live, but that its justification was to be found only if men lived nobly. So (and I believe that in this thought I have the full agreement of all those who have taken part in these conversations), the international organization should be brought into existence in order that nations may be saved from destruction; but it also will only be justified if through the years all humanity is enabled by it to find the way to a better and nobler life.

At noon on 9 October 1944 the text of the proposals that the four groups had agreed upon was issued simultaneously in Washington, London, Moscow, and Chungking. The following day Dumbarton Oaks began its return to the Byzantine considerations of its normal occupants.

During the year following the end of the war, Dumbarton Oaks began to assume its present form as a research center for Byzantine studies. In the course of February 1946 the National Defense Research Committee vacated the space it had occupied during the war, and by the end of the year the wings fronting on 32nd Street had been rehabilitated for the return of the collection. At this time an additional corridor was built along the north wall of the music room to permit direct access from the public entrance on 32nd Street to the stair hall of the main house without passing through the music room. This addition, which increased the flexibility of the ground plan, provided as well wall space for exhibition purposes. The research library, constantly growing, began to flow into various parts of the main house. Adjacent buildings on the property were converted to provide quarters for professors, fellows, and the superintendent.

The full development of the Center for Byzantine Studies, which is an integral part of Harvard University although five hundred miles away from Cambridge, in the years since 1946 led to constant transformations of the interior of Dumbarton Oaks. But although the upper floors and basement have been radically altered to provide for a growing library and the scholars who use it, the first floor rooms have retained their architectural character. The music room, which accommo-

dates the five or six public lectures on Byzantine themes that are annually given by visiting scholars, not only looks much as it did when built,
but continues to be used for the purposes for which Mr. and Mrs. Bliss
had designed it.

At the end of the war, a small group of persons particularly interested in chamber music took steps to assure the continuation of the
concerts that had been so agreeable a feature of Dumbarton Oaks as a
private house. "The Friends of Music at Dumbarton Oaks" were organized in the autumn of 1946 with the purpose of adding to the musical
repertory of Washington by presenting chamber music in a setting
reminiscent of that for which it had originally been composed. Each
year since then, four or more concerts have been presented in the music
room. Although Igor Stravinsky, Francois Poulenc, and Aaron Copeland
have conducted their own compositions, usually the programs present
the chamber music of the eighteenth or earlier centuries for which the
setting is so suitable. Alexander Schneider, Wanda Landowska, Ralph
Kirkpatrick, and Rudolph Serkin have performed there on various
occasions, while Joan Sutherland and Leontyne Price have sung. There
has also been an extraordinary variety of chamber music groups over
the years, from both the United States and Europe. The American Opera
Society, the New York Pro Musica Motet Choir and Woodwind En-
semble, the New York Chamber Soloists, and the Philadelphia Woodwind Quintet have appeared there on various occasions, as have chamber orchestras conducted by Alexander Schneider or Paul Callaway.
European groups have included the Boyd Neel Orchestra, the Lucerne
Festival group, I Musici, Orchestra San Pietro of Naples, Società
Corelli, Solisti di Zagreb, Stuttgart Chamber Orchestra, Trio di Trieste,
Vienna Octet, the Virtuosi di Roma, and the Zurich Little Symphony.

Even during the war, when the Byzantine Collection was in storage,
purchases of desirable objects were made by Harvard and gifts were
received from various friends. These additions greatly increased in
number when the collection was once again on public exhibition. In
1947 G. Howland Shaw presented his collection of Byzantine coins; the
following year the Hayford Peirce collection, consisting of more than
four thousand related coins, was purchased. Systematically over the
past two decades the Dumbarton Oaks collection of Byzantine coins has

been augmented until it is now one of the largest and most complete in existence. This effort was often aided by anonymous gifts from Mr. and Mrs. Bliss. In addition to the constant interest that they maintained in the growth of the numismatic collection, they continued to enrich Dumbarton Oaks with important Byzantine objects when these became available in the market. To commemorate their 44th wedding anniversary, they gave a fourth-century marble Byzantine relief of Christ healing the blind man, and on their 45th an amethyst intaglio with a standing figure of Christ, probably of the fifth or sixth century.

The amethyst intaglio has a particular poignancy, for the gift was made not only in gratitude for the donors' own anniversary but in memory of their friend Royall Tyler, who had just died. That remarkable scholar, whose death was as great a loss to learning as it was to his friends, is also significantly commemorated at Dumbarton Oaks by the sixth-century silver chalice bearing an inscription from the liturgy of St. John Chrysostom. This vessel, which had been found in the same treasure at Riha in Syria that contained the Bliss's paten and flabellum, was for thirty years in Tyler's own collection. In 1955 it was given in his memory to Dumbarton Oaks by his widow and his son, William Royall Tyler. Thus three superb and closely related objects are once more reunited to perpetuate a friendship that played a great part in the genesis of Dumbarton Oaks.

To celebrate the fiftieth anniversary of their wedding, on 14 April 1958, Mrs. Bliss gave to Dumbarton Oaks a gold and blue enamel cross of the sixth century, with the Greek inscription "Light, Life" on the reverse, while Mr. Bliss gave an important gold medallion of Constantius II (323–361). In graceful reciprocation, Dumbarton Oaks arranged a concert in the music room that day under the direction of Mademoiselle Nadia Boulanger.

On Sunday, 31 October 1965, at a celebration commemorating the twenty-fifth anniversary of the Dumbarton Oaks Research Library and Collection, Miss Sirarpie der Nersessian, Henri Focillon Professor of Byzantine Art and Archaeology, *Emerita*, spoke at the morning session on "Scholarship in Byzantine Art and Archaeology, 1940–1965." In the afternoon, Romilly J. H. Jenkins, Professor of Byzantine History and Literature at Dumbarton Oaks, discussed "Scholarship in Byzantine History and Literature, 1940–1965." The contributions that the Dumbarton Oaks Center for Byzantine Studies has made during this quarter century will be recorded, as I indicated in the Foreword, in Professor Ernst Kitzinger's forthcoming book. It is there, rather than here, that one will find the record of the true harvest that has been reaped at Dumbarton Oaks in the years that the place has belonged to Harvard University.

The house and grounds, with their subtle integration of many arts, continue to furnish a provocative setting for the scholarly thought of those who carry forward the investigations of the Center for Byzantine Studies. But in addition to this, which is their primary purpose, they annually give pleasure and refreshment to thousands of visitors, who are grateful to the founders for creating and to Harvard University for maintaining this remarkable portion of "America's most civilized square mile."

North of Dumbarton Oaks, on a bluff directly above the ravine that was in 1940 given by Mr. and Mrs. Bliss to the Federal Government as Dumbarton Oaks Park, stands a related outpost of Harvard University, the Center for Hellenic Studies, recently created through the generosity of Paul Mellon and the Old Dominion Foundation. This Center annually brings to the District of Columbia a number of young Greek scholars, who often find their way to Dumbarton Oaks, even though the two institutions are independently administered. There is pleasing intellectual symmetry in having two Harvard University centers, the one concerned with the culture of classical Greece, the other with its Byzantine metamorphosis — both created through singularly imaginative private generosity — on opposite sides of a beautiful ravine in the capital of the United States "to clarify an ever changing present and to inform the future with wisdom."

CHAPTER IX

Pre-Columbian Art and
the Garden Library

IT has been noted in an earlier chapter that Robert and Mildred Bliss, in giving Dumbarton Oaks to Harvard University, intended that what they had created should become the basis of an ever-growing research institution rather than a static crystallization of an owner's taste, like Mrs. Gardner's Fenway Court in Boston or Sir John Soane's Museum in Lincoln's Inn Fields. But when two incurable collectors give away what they have so painstakingly assembled, it by no means follows that they simultaneously relinquish their love of the chase. Two wings that were added to Dumbarton Oaks in 1963, through Mrs. Bliss's generosity, symbolize the extent of her husband's and her separate collecting in quite different fields in the years following their gift of the place to Harvard, above and beyond their continuing interest in the growth of the Byzantine Collection.

When the United States entered World War II, the Blisses were living in Montecito, California. But being constitutionally unable, after a third of a century of public service, to eat lotus in wartime, they returned to Washington in 1942, where Robert Bliss was given a post as Consultant to the Secretary of State. They bought a house at 1537 28th Street in Georgetown, small in comparison to what they had earlier created a few blocks to the northwest, but with a garden containing one great beech tree. In February 1944, with a change of title, Mr. Bliss was assigned for special work as representative of the Department of State with the Office of Strategic Services, which occupied him fully until the end of the war. Thereafter much of his time was devoted to the duties of a trustee or officer of numerous institutions, including the American Federation of Arts, the American Museum of Natural History, the American-Scandinavian Foundation, the Foreign Service Educational Foundation, the Carnegie Institution of Washington, and the National Trust for Historic Preservation. In 1939 he had been elected an Overseer of Harvard University for a six-year term, and he had served on the Administrative Committee of Dumbarton Oaks from the beginning.

The secretary of the Harvard class of 1900, in sending out questionnaires in preparation for periodical reports, invariably included space for what he inelegantly called "Hobbies." In 1945 Robert Bliss concluded his entry with the laconic but accurate final paragraph: "My hobbies? My wife and Dumbarton Oaks!" But for the fiftieth anniversary report, he extended his remarks to include

one that takes not an inconsiderable part of my time; that is what I call "Indigenous Art of the Americas." About forty years ago I became interested in the sculpture and artifacts in general of the various pre-Columbian cultures of Mexico, Central America, and the west coast of South America. At that time few, if any, of our *art* museums had on display these objects, which were only made available to the public in museums of natural history as part of their archaeological finds. To me, many of the pieces I saw had artistic significance and also revealed remarkable craftsmanship. So I began to collect, buying only pieces which appealed to me as objects of art. After moving to Washington I was able to give more time to this increasingly absorbing interest. It was then that I began to try to impress upon others the importance to the history of art, of the stylized and powerful sculpture of the early inhabitants of the western hemisphere. To this end I loaned objects to various museums, and finally organized a special exhibition at the Santa Barbara Art Museum in 1941, during a convalescence from a serious surgical operation. Today many art museums throughout the country have fine displays of pre-Columbian art. What I have amassed is a small collection of carved jadeite and other hard stones, of gold, silver, and bronze objects, with a few examples of ceramics and Peruvian textiles; these are now on loan at the National Gallery of Art (Mellon Gallery) in Washington.

In 1947 his friends David E. Finley, then Director of the National Gallery of Art, and John Walker, then Chief Curator, placed at Mr.

Bliss's disposal wall cases in a room on the ground floor of the National Gallery that leads visitors from the Constitution Avenue entrance to the galleries used for temporary exhibitions. This was a singularly appropriate place for missionary work on behalf of pre-Columbian art, for thousands of visitors had to pass by the cases containing Mr. Bliss's collection, whether they had any interest in the subject or not. It also was a severe test of the artistic interest of the objects, for the standards of the National Gallery of Art, both as to quality and as to methods of display, are of the highest. There the collection remained on loan for some fifteen years, bringing to thousands of visitors their first acquaintance with this dramatic manifestation of the art of the American continents.

A handbook entitled *Indigenous Art of the Americas, Collection of Robert Woods Bliss* was published in 1947 by the National Gallery of Art when the objects were first displayed there. Ten years later the Phaidon Press Ltd. in London published a sumptuous small folio volume, *Robert Woods Bliss Collection, Pre-Columbian Art*, with numerous color plates, the text and critical analyses being by Dr. Samuel Kirkland Lothrop and Miss Joy Mahler of the Peabody Museum at Harvard University and Dr. William F. Foshag, Head Curator of the Department of Geology of the United States National Museum. A second edition was required in 1958, while Italian and German editions were published in 1959.

Robert Bliss died on 19 April 1962, five days after he and his wife had observed their 54th wedding anniversary. As he had bequeathed the Pre-Columbian Collection to Dumbarton Oaks, it was soon after his death removed there from the National Gallery of Art, and steps were taken to provide for its appropriate exhibition. This was achieved by the addition of a new wing, to the north of the Byzantine Collection gallery. Designed by Philip Johnson, it was completed and first opened to visitors on 10 December 1963. This charming building, circular in plan, with small galleries around a central courtyard, in which a fountain splashes, defies description. It suggests the kind of octagonal rococo conceit that one might find in the garden of an eighteenth-century palace, translated into rich but severe contemporary materials, entirely without ornament, with a liberal use of plate glass. Although radically different from all earlier construction at Dumbarton Oaks, it avoids the common contemporary sin against architectural charity — that of being wilfully disharmonious with older neighbors — because of its skilful placing. As this wing projects into a heavily planted area of the gardens, rich in evergreens and large rhododendrons, it is all but invisible from the exterior. From no normal vantage point in the street, gardens, or house does one realize that it is there. From the inside, however, one looks out into rich thickets that provide a kind of jungle backdrop for the objects, which are displayed with lucite pedestals and (where necessary) cases, that are contrived to be as nearly invisible as possible. Thus a mood is created that takes the pre-Columbian objects into a world infinitely remote, and all their own. But it has to be seen to be believed; no photograph or description will convey it. Were-jaguars, black basalt feathered serpents, porphyry coiled rattlesnakes, gold monkeys, eagles, and deer surround such awesome Aztec deities as Tlazolteotl, goddess of childbirth, agonizing in labor, or Xipe, clad in the human skin of one of the innumerable victims sacrificed to him. Although the objects are often beautiful in themselves, in their particular way, they evoke a brutal and terrifying world, from which one can happily escape, merely by walking through a passage, to Greece and the more hopeful Byzantine view of eternity. In a moment one can exchange the bloodthirsty Xipe for the beneficent Hestia Polyolbos and the agonizing squatting Tlazolteotl for the serene Virgin Hodegetria and, by going only a few more steps, find oneself in the present day beauty of the gardens, to which the writ of Aztec gods never extends. The strength of importations and borrowings in the cultural life of peoples has never been better demonstrated than here, for though the pre-Columbian wing contains the indigenous art of our own western continents, these objects seem the strange visions of nightmares. Although Americans, we are on more familiar ground in Byzantium than in Teotihuacán. "Indigenismo," like the "frontier fallacy," by which certain critics praise only those elements in American life and arts that they believe to be native to this continent, is an unduly limiting and restrictive concept.

With the acquisition of this collection, the Trustees for Harvard University appointed an Advisory Committee for Pre-Columbian Art, of which Professor John Otis Brew, Director of the Peabody Museum,

Harvard University, is Chairman. Dr. Michael D. Coe, who joined the Dumbarton Oaks staff as Advisor for Pre-Columbian Art, gave a public lecture, "The Beginning of Mesoamerican Civilization," on 7 February 1964, that was the first pre-Columbian offering in a series that had hitherto been wholly Byzantine. The illustrated *Handbook of the Robert Woods Bliss Collection of Pre-Columbian Art*, published on the opening of the new wing, lists 425 items. Four of these were given by Mrs. Bliss, four by Dr. Lothrop, one by John Wise, and one by Dr. Coe, and two pieces were purchased in 1963; the remaining 413 objects had all been collected by Robert Bliss. This is a good example of the danger of an incurable collector going walking in Paris with Royall Tyler; so for that matter is the Byzantine Collection, although there Mrs. Bliss occupied the role of joint consul with her husband.

With the Pre-Columbian Collection was received a library, assembled by Mr. Bliss, of approximately 1,400 volumes, in addition to 700 pamphlets and reprints, to which some 250 items were added in the first year that it was installed at Dumbarton Oaks.

No collection of any kind is of serious use unless it is in the charge of competent scholars, equipped with an adequate research library. It was soon recognized at Dumbarton Oaks that the gardens required learned men and books quite as urgently as the Byzantine and Pre-Columbian Collections. Plants and trees are a great deal more troublesome than inanimate objects; first they are too small, but soon they are too big. While some are short-lived, even the hardiest may be uprooted by the boisterous antics of hurricanes, or killed by disease or the eccentricities of an especially rigorous winter. Moreover, few people are able to visualize the future growth of different plants in relation to each other and their surroundings, and thus take appropriate action at the right moment. When a tree has become a fine specimen, it takes fortitude to cut it down, even though it may obviously be defeating the purpose of design for which it was originally planted. Thus constant vigilance, fortified by knowledge, is essential to prevent a well designed garden from growing into a romantic shambles. Lanning Roper, writing of Dumbarton Oaks, observed in 1959, "Mr. and Mrs. Bliss have with vision realized the difficulty of trying to freeze a garden scheme. Trees and hedges have a life-span; blights, diseases and cyclones take their toll. A body of experienced experts must advise. Mrs. Bliss keeps in the closest touch with the garden and with this advisory group. There are certain new schemes which she hopes may in time become reality for the instruction of future gardeners." Thus in 1955 the Trustees for Harvard University appointed a Garden Advisory Committee, originally under the chairmanship of Michael Rapuano, to serve the same function for the gardens that the Board of Scholars does for the Center for Byzantine Studies. This committee has met two or three times a year ever since to study the future of the gardens and to recommend professional appointments to fellowships in connection with them.

In the academic year 1954–55, Lester Collins, formerly of the School of Architecture, Harvard University, was in residence at Dumbarton Oaks as Visiting Lecturer on Landscape Architecture and Design. From 1956 to 1959 Ralph E. Griswold, the distinguished Pittsburgh landscape architect, held the first Dumbarton Oaks appointment as Research Fellow in Landscape Architecture, during which he completed a study of the geographical history of landscape architecture from the earliest times to the eighteenth century, with particular emphasis on interpreting the role of individuals in the history of garden art. This enabled him to travel abroad to do research, as well as to write quietly at Dumbarton Oaks when in residence. Mr. Griswold was the landscape architect responsible for the planting of the Agora in Athens, and after the completion of his fellowship he served for a time as Professional Adviser for the Dumbarton Oaks gardens.

In 1956, the year of Mr. Griswold's initial appointment, two Summer Garden Fellowships were created for college undergraduates, chosen by a special committee of the American Society of Landscape Architects, to study at Dumbarton Oaks and to work in close conjunction with Mr. Matthew Kearney, the Superintendent of Gardens and Grounds. These have since been continued, with the number increased to three from 1962. In various years Junior and Senior Research Fellows in Garden Design and in Landscape Architecture have been in residence, some of them brought from Europe for the purpose.

In the late nineteen forties, the garden library at Dumbarton Oaks consisted of some nine hundred volumes, many of which were rare, and some two thousand prints of flowers and local birds. These were housed, with other rare books and manuscripts left at Dumbarton Oaks by Mrs. Bliss, in the drawing room of the house, which was in 1948 formally designated by the Trustees for Harvard University as the Founders' Room. During the fifties, Mrs. Bliss devoted her collecting energies to the rapid enlargement and improvement of the garden library. Through her own gifts, and those that she inspired, it had grown by 1955 to over three thousand volumes, including many rare works of the fifteenth and sixteenth centuries, and such modern reference tools as the International Code of Botanical Nomenclature. In 1960, when new cataloguing and classification was undertaken, there were six thousand volumes, and two years later the number had increased to ten thousand.

The additions of these years included such early botanical works and treatises on the medicinal use of plants as the *Hortus Sanitatis* of 1491, the *Materia Medica* of Dioscorides of 1499, original water color tracings of the Badianus herbal of 1552, and first editions of Gerard's *Herball* (1597), Monardes' *Historia Medecinal* (1574) — with the contemporary English translation entitled *Joyfull Newes out of the New-found Worlde* — and Christoval Acosta's *Tractado de las Drogas* (Burgos, 1578). Treatises on country life, agriculture, fruit growing and horticulture run from Petrus de Crescentiis, *Il libro della agricultura* (Venice, 1495), through William Lawson, *A New Orchard and Garden* (London, 1653), Gervase Markham, *A Way to Get Wealth; Six Treatises on Gardening and Husbandry* (London, 1653), Antoine Mizault and Vinet Elie, *La Maison Champestre* (Paris, 1607), Batty Langley, *Pomona or the Fruit Garden Illustrated* (London, 1729), to a copy once owned by George Washington of Thomas Mawe and John Abercrombie, *The Universal Gardener and Botanist* (London, 1778).

Works of eighteenth-century naturalists were purchased, like Mark Catesby's *The Natural History of North Carolina, Florida, and the Bahama Islands* (London, 1731), and treatises like Curtis's *Flora Londinensis*, Rabel's *Theatrum Florae*, Besler's *Hortus Eystettensis*, Gallesio's *Pomona italiana*, and Mueller's *Illustratio Systematis Sexualis Linnaei*.

Architectural books of the eighteenth century, like Colin Campbell's *Vitruvius Brittanicus*, James Gibbs's, *A book of Architecture, Containing Designs of Buildings and Ornaments*, Charles-Etienne Briseux's *L'Art de batir les maisons de campagne,* and Gabriel Martin Dumont's *Receuil de plusieurs parties d'Architecture de differents maîtres tant d'Italia que de France* were procured for the light that they might throw upon gardens, for the particular specialty of the collection is the illustration of the evolution of garden design and ornament.

Even after the installation of shelves on all its walls, the Founders' Room was no longer adequate to house the garden library. Consequently a wing was added, to the south of the 32nd Street entrance, for its proper accommodation. The new Garden Library, which was opened late in 1963, was designed by Frederic Rhinelander King. It fits its purpose as admirably as does Philip Johnson's Pre-Columbian Gallery, but as the purpose of the two wings is totally different, so is their architecture. The main library is a tall, exquisitely elegant, rectangular room, of French inspiration, with long windows, mirrors, and crystal chandeliers; it is divided into alcoves by tall bookcases, capable of receiving eighteenth century folios. In spirit it brings the gardens indoors. The corridor that leads from the 32nd Street entrance is lined with wall cases for the exhibition of books and prints. There are also, on this floor and in the basement, offices and work rooms for the library staff, and stack space.

The Garden Library extends into the former South Lawn, near the 32nd and R Streets corner of the property. Unlike the Pre-Columbian Gallery, which nestles almost invisibly in its jungle of evergreens and rhododendrons, this wing is seen in relation to the main driveway and entrance facade of the house. Consequently Mrs. Bliss and the landscape architect Miss Ruth Havey have been engaged in devising planting, subtly designed curving brick paths on various levels, and new uses of garden ornaments, that will soon make it seem from the gardens as integral a part of the place as it already does when one is indoors. Thus the process of planning and experimenting with garden design that began with Mrs. Farrand and Mrs. Bliss close to forty-five years ago is still going on.

The gardens inevitably change in detail. The transfer twenty-five years ago from the intimately personal care of a resident owner to the necessarily impersonal but enduring custody of a university required certain simplifications in detail, but brought no marked changes in the main units of the plan. Individual elements over the years sometimes have to be replaced, but without violence to the original design. As examples, the great purple beech, around which the terrace of that name was planned, died, but the young silver-stemmed beech that was substituted for it is rapidly growing to fill its appointed place. Similarly, when the plantings of box that encircled the Ellipse became overgrown and out of scale, they were removed to make way for a double line of pleached hornbeams that formed what Mr. Lanning Roper called an "aerial hedge." Also, as inanimate elements in the garden design have deteriorated with age, they have been replaced in materials better able to resist weather in future years. Thus the wooden gates of the driveway entrances from R Street have been replaced with wrought-iron ones of a new design, with the symbolical sheaves of wheat highlighted by gilding. Similarly, when Allyn Cox's mural paintings of Diana and Actaeon in the loggia by the swimming pool deteriorated from exposure to winter weather, they were, in 1965, reproduced in mosaic.

Some entire areas of the gardens have been redesigned in recent years. Mr. Lanning Roper thus described the alteration of the Urn Terrace, which was planned around a stone copy of an eighteenth-century Italian terracotta that had been considered too fragile for the Washington climate.

This urn originally stood in the centre of a formal box-edged parterre but in time the box grew beyond bounds and this scheme was replaced by a baroque pebble garden. Attractive beds of dwarf shamrock-leaved ivy outlined in brick surround the intricately shaped pebbled areas and in the centre the swag embellished column for the urn rises from further baroque patterns of Doria stone and coloured pebbles. Round the outside box-bordered beds of paeonies, columbines and irises partially screen the open work brick balustrade along which wistarias and winter jasmine are trained. The fascinating baroque scrolls and patterns are the work of the landscape architect Miss Ruth Havey.

Miss Havey's facility in draughting garden ornaments and designs first became known to Mrs. Bliss through the innumerable delightful thumbnail sketches she submitted to Mrs. Farrand in the early stages of planning the Dumbarton Oaks gardens. Thus gradually Mrs. Bliss and Miss Havey came to enjoy each other's tentative jottings of ideas,

out of which developed the designs for various benches, seats, and ornaments. When Mrs. Farrand's age and increasing frailty finally forced her
to retire, Miss Havey and Mrs. Bliss carried on. The most dramatic
recent innovation is the transformation of the disused tennis court into
a Pebble Garden, far larger and bolder than the work in similar materials
on the Urn Terrace. Here Miss Havey, working closely with Mrs. Bliss,
achieved striking baroque swirls and curves that are extraordinarily
agreeable when seen through shallow pools of water from the terraces
above them. Moreover the "pebbles" require nothing like the care and
feeding of living plants.

At any season, even midwinter, the gardens of Dumbarton Oaks enrich the spirit and stimulate the imagination. In wandering through
them, the visitor is appropriately reminded of those who had a part in
their achievement. It is characteristic of the place and its creators to
find an inscription reading:

WILLIAM JAMES GRAY
SEPT. 14, 1882–DEC. 31, 1957
SUPERINTENDENT OF DUMBARTON OAKS
1922   1957

THE TREES AND PLANTS RESPONDED TO HIS CARE
HIS SUBORDINATES FOLLOWED HIM GLADLY
BECAUSE HE WAS JUST
HIS EMPLOYERS TRUSTED HIM FOR HIS FAIR-MINDEDNESS
LOYALTY AND COMMON-SENSE
UNFAILINGLY COURTEOUS AND
HUMOROUSLY PHILOSOPHICAL
HE WON THE REGARD OF ALL WHO KNEW HIM
AND AN ENDURING PLACE IN THEIR MEMORY

THE DIGNITY OF HIS SPIRIT IS GATHERED INTO
THE SHADOWS OF THESE GARDENS HE LOVED SO WELL

And in the center of the panel in the terrace balustrade overlooking the
pool is another inscription, carved as a surprise for Beatrix Farrand:

SOMNIA SUB PATULIS VIDEBANT NASCIENTIA RAMIS
SIDERA FAUSTA FERANT OMNIA ET USQUE BONA

TESTIMONIO AMICITIAE
BEATRICIS FARRAND
NEC ILLORUM IMMEMORES QUI POSTERO AEVO
VITAS VERITATI ERVENDAE IMPENDERINT
HANC TABELLAM POSUERUNT
ROBERTUS WOODS BLISS UXORQUE MILDRED

It is equally typical of the place that if a visitor should happen upon Robert Bliss's grave in a quiet corner of one of the garden terraces, he would find it marked only by the name and dates of birth and death. Unlike Dorseys, Beverleys, Calhouns, and the other itinerants who followed them, an owner of Dumbarton Oaks is staying here for all time and eternity.

Illustrations

Proſpectus Arcis Regiæ BRITANNODUNENSIS ab Occidente. Their Maties Castle of DUMBRITTON from the West

The Rock of Dumbarton on the River Clyde, Scotland
From John Slezer, Theatrum Scotiae, 1693

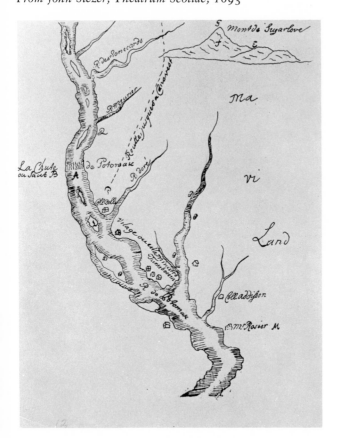

Rock of Dumbarton on the Potomac River, Maryland, patented in 1703 by Colonel Ninian Beall

Environs shown in Baron Christopher de Graffenreid's map of 1712

Thomas Beall of George (1748–1819), grandson of Colonel Ninian Beall, who inherited a portion of Rock of Dumbarton in 1780

From a miniature in the Maryland Historical Society

Anne (Orme) Beall (1752–1827), wife of Thomas Beall of George

From a miniature in the Maryland Historical Society

Robert Beverley (1769–1843) of Blandfield, Essex County, Virginia, who bought the house in 1805 and named it Acrolophos

From a portrait by St. Memin in the Corcoran Gallery of Art

William Hammond Dorsey (1764–1818), builder of the house that became Dumbarton Oaks

From a painting attributed to George William West in the Maryland Historical Society

House built by William Hammond Dorsey at Rock of Dumbarton in 1800

From the earliest known photograph, taken about 1860, after the addition of a wooden porch

Orangery added to Acrolophos by Robert Beverley

From the earliest known photograph, taken about 1860, which shows the original roof

Orangery at Wye House, Talbot County, Maryland, the home of Colonel Edward Lloyd, brother-in-law of Robert Beverley

From a photograph by E. M. Pickering in the Historic American Building Survey, Library of Congress

James Edward Calhoun
(1798–1899), naval offi-
cer, brother-in-law of John
Caldwell Calhoun, who ac-
quired Acrolophos in 1823
*Courtesy of Francis de Sales
Dundas, Esq., Staunton, Virginia*

Floride (Bonneau) Colhoun,
widow of John Ewing Col-
houn and mother of James
Edward Calhoun

*From a portrait in the At-
lanta Art Association*

John Caldwell Calhoun (1782–1850), Vice President of the United States, who lived in the house, which he called Oakly

From a portrait by Charles Bird King in the Corcoran Gallery of Art

Floride Colhoun, wife of John Caldwell Calhoun

From a miniature by Charles Fraser in Fort Hill, the old home of John Caldwell Calhoun, courtesy of Mrs. E. W. Cooke, Clemson College, South Carolina

Major Christopher Van Deventer, Chief Clerk of the War Department, who rented Oakly from the Calhouns

From a portrait by John Trumbull, courtesy of Christopher Van Deventer, Esq., III, Nashville, Tennessee

Sally (Birckhead) Van Deventer, wife of Major Christopher Van Deventer

Courtesy of Christopher Van Deventer, Esq., III, Nashville, Tennessee

View of Georgetown in 1855

From a lithograph by E. Sachse & Co. in the Library of Congress

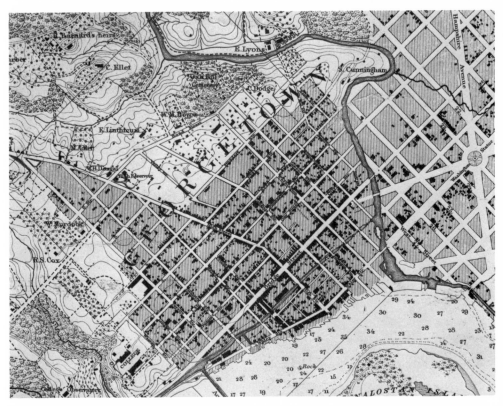

Portion of Boschke's Topographical Map 1856–59 showing the location of the Linthicum property above Georgetown

From Office of Chief of Engineers Headquarters Map File, Map F69, in the National Archives

Edward Magruder Linthicum (1797–1869), Georgetown hardware dealer, who bought the house in 1846 and named it The Oaks

From a portrait by Henry Ulke in the Linthicum Institute

Kate Mitchell (Linthicum) Dent (1837–1862), wife of Josiah Dent, with The Oaks in the background, before Linthicum alterations

Courtesy of Miss Mary Catherine Dent

South facade of The Oaks as altered by Edward Magruder Linthicum
From a photograph of about 1890, courtesy of Mrs. Walter G. Peter

North facade of The Oaks as altered by Edward Magruder Linthicum
From a photograph of about 1890

South facade of The Oaks in the late nineteenth century
From a photograph in the Columbia Historical Society

The Orangery showing the enlarged hip roof as altered by Edward Magruder
Linthicum
From a photograph by Schutz, Washington, D.C.

Edward Linthicum Dent (1862–1899), who divided the estate into building lots
Courtesy of Miss Mary Catherine Dent

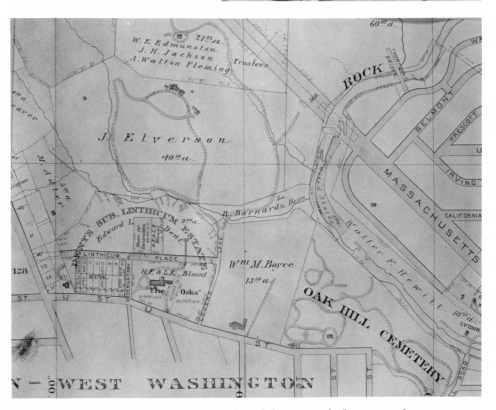

Map showing Edward Linthicum Dent's subdivision of the original 22-acre tract
From Griffith M. Hopkins, Real Estate Plat Book, vol. 3 (1894), in the Library of Congress

Colonel Henry Fitch Blount
(1829–1917), who bought
the house in 1891 and later
other portions of the original estate

*Courtesy of Walter E. Blount,
Esq., Florida City, Florida*

Lucia (Eames) Blount, wife
of Colonel Henry Fitch
Blount and a charter mem-
ber of the D.A.R.

*Courtesy of Walter E. Blount,
Esq., Florida City, Florida*

Elizabeth Blount reading to her sister Mary in the "Ferdinand and Isabella chairs"

Courtesy of Mrs. Eugene R. Shippen, Winter Park, Florida

Stage of Little Theatre, with seating capacity of 200, added in top floor of The Oaks by the Blounts

Courtesy of Mrs. Eugene R. Shippen, Winter Park, Florida

South facade of The Oaks showing the Blounts' enlargement over the porch
and some of the surviving original 12-pane windows with counter-sunk
panels between them

From a late nineteenth century photograph

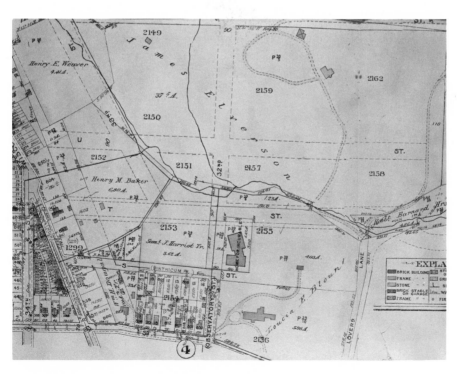

Map showing changes in original 22-acre tract

*From George William Baisted, Real Estate Atlas, vol. 3 (1919), in the
Library of Congress*

Mildred Barnes Bliss, wife of Robert Woods Bliss

From a drawing by Albert Sterner, 1908, in Dumbarton Oaks

Royall Tyler

Oval Room
From a photograph by Sigurd Fischer

East staircase in the Long Gallery
From a photograph by Sigurd Fischer

South facade of Dumbarton Oaks
From a photograph taken in the winter of 1925–26

Drawing room as originally designed with Hubert Robert panels
From a photograph by Sigurd Fischer

Bay window of drawing room
From a photograph by Sigurd Fischer

Entrance to music room with mural paintings by Allyn Cox

From a photograph by Sigurd Fischer

Music room looking southwest
From a photograph by Sigurd Fischer

Music room looking northeast
From a photograph by Sigurd Fischer

South facade of Dumbarton Oaks

North facade of Dumbarton Oaks

Aquarius Fountain in Star Garden
From a photograph by Stewart Brothers

Green Garden
From a photograph by Stewart Brothers

Swimming pool and loggia
From a photograph by Stewart Brothers

Staircase with fountain between Green Garden and swimming pool

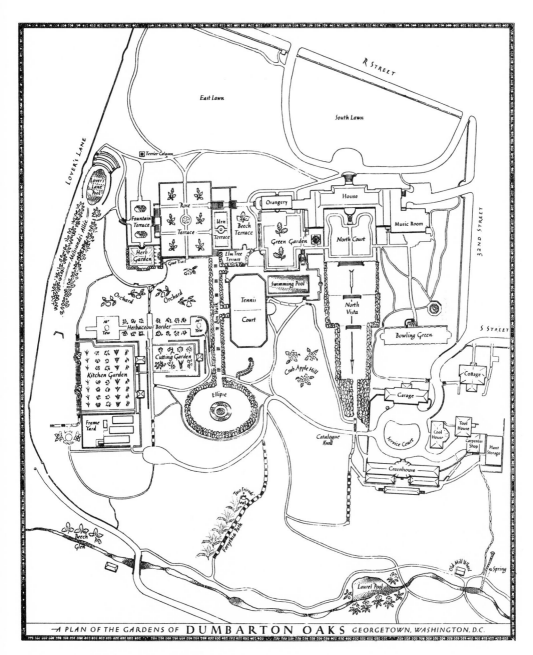

Plan of the gardens of Dumbarton Oaks in 1935
From a drawing by Rudolph Ruzicka

Urn Terrace looking north

From a photograph by Stewart Brothers

Rose Terrace looking west to Orangery

From a photograph by Stewart Brothers

Fountain Terrace looking west

South gate to Fountain Terrace

From a photograph by Stewart Brothers

Du Cerceau Arbor in Herb (later Pot) Garden

From a photograph by Stewart Brothers

Herbaceous border looking west in 1932

Herbaceous border looking north through gates toward cutting and kitchen gardens

Arbor below kitchen garden

Lover's Lane Pool

Box Walk looking north toward the Ellipse

Service court looking northwest in 1932

From a photograph by Stewart Brothers

Mildred and Robert Bliss in the music room

32nd Street entrance to the Library and Collection
From a photograph by Sigurd Fischer

Wing for the Pre-Columbian Collection
From photographs by Ezra Stoller

View from the Veracruz Room into the Post-Classic Room in the Pre-Columbian Wing

Interiors of the Garden Library

Beatrix Farrand inscription

Exterior of the Garden Library

Index